Creative Science

Also available:

The Teaching of Science in Primary Schools
Wynne Harlen OBE and Anne Qualter
1-84312-132-8

Active Assessment
Thinking, Learning and Assessment in Science
Stuart Naylor, Brenda Keogh and Anne Goldsworthy
1-84312-145-X

Science 3–11
A Guide for Teachers
Alan Howe, Dan Davies and Kendra McMahon
1-84312-319-3

Creative Teaching
Science in the Early Years and Primary Classroom
Ann Oliver
1-84312-259-6

Science Knowledge for Primary Teachers
Understanding the Science in the QCA Scheme
Linda Gillard
1-84312-188-3

Meeting SEN in the Curriculum – Science
Carol Holden
1-84312-159-X

Meeting the Needs of Your Most Able Students in Science
Tim Alderman
1-84312-277-4

Science and ICT in the Primary School
A Creative Approach to Big Ideas
John Meadows
1-84312-120-4

Access to Science
Curriculum Planning and Practical Activities for Pupils with Learning
Difficulties
Claire Marvin and Chris Stokoe
1-85346-917-3

Creative Science

Achieving the WOW factor with 5–11 year olds

Rosemary Feasey

David Fulton Publishers

David Fulton Publishers
2 Park Square, Milton Park, Abingdon, Oxon OX14 4RN

270 Madison Avenue, New York, NY 10016

Transferred to digital printing

David Fulton Publishers is an imprint of the Taylor & Francis Group, an infoma business

Copyright © Rosemary Feasey 2005

British Library Cataloguing in Publication Data
A catalogue record for this book is available from the British Library.

ISBN: 1 84312 305 3

Typeset by RefineCatch Limited, Bungay, Suffolk

Contents

For Steve

Preface

Creative science teaching can produce a 'Wow!' response from the teacher as he or she enjoys a lively and exciting lesson and the equally creative and awesome responses from the children as they are 'wowed' by that teaching and their own learning. More subtle is the quiet 'Wow' of satisfaction when the teacher or the child reflects on their accomplishments. Supporting teachers, trainee teachers, consultants, advisers, inspectors and indeed anyone who is involved with primary science, in achieving the 'Wow!' factor is the main aim of this book, through involving the reader in considering the role of creativity in the primary science curriculum.

One of the main themes of the book is the centrality of children's ideas about creativity. A typically constructivist approach was taken in eliciting children's understanding of the nature of creativity and children's perceptions of their own creativity. What emerged from their ideas is that children can understand creativity and become partners in developing their own creative abilities and potential.

Each chapter offers vignettes and examples from classrooms, where the teachers and children have been involved in creative teaching and learning episodes. Alongside each of these 'teaching and learning stories' is an analysis of how each one supported the development of creativity in science.

At the end of each chapter there is a plan for a creative activity in science which, alongside the ideas in each chapter, I hope readers will feel enthused to use with children in schools.

Most importantly, this book aims to celebrate creativity in science through examples of children's verbal responses and their written work. Children have enormous creative potential which we should aim to develop with enthusiasm and anticipation, as well as celebrate. Central to this book is the idea that it is both the teacher's right to be creative in their teaching, and the duty of the teacher to develop children's creative potential in science.

Our challenge (and it is an exciting one) as teachers is to offer children creative approaches to teaching and learning and allow each child to become a partner in developing his or her creative potential, so that they can enjoy science and, in doing so, make sense of their world.

Acknowledgements

I am indebted to the many teachers I have met during in-service sessions who have talked to me about their own efforts to be creative in their science teaching. Some of these episodes have been used in this book. My thanks also go to the teachers who completed research questionnaires and allowed me to access some of their thinking on creativity in science.

I would like to give special thanks to the children and the teachers from the following schools and others who have offered activities, children's work and inspiration:

Anne Goldsworthy

Archbishop Runcie First School, Newcastle Upon Tyne

Barbara Higginbotham – Data Harvest

Bukky Yusof – Hackney LEA

Chris Meikle – teacher

Ruth Tait Bridges – teacher

Sadyia Kasmi – Hackney LEA

St Thomas Moore Primary School, Durham

Waverley Primary School, Newcastle Upon Tyne

Westgate Hill Primary School, Newcastle Upon Tyne

Wingrove Primary School, Newcastle Upon Tyne

Children's names, where used, have been changed.

My heartfelt and sincere thanks go to my good friends Roy and Anne Phipps who so kindly read through the draft manuscript and offered suggestions with such grace and patience.

What is creativity?

 Creativity helps you know more stuff about what you might want to do when you're a grown-up.

(Ben, age 9)

A shared understanding of creativity is elusive. Most people, when asked, would be able to name a creative person and what some of the characteristics of a creative person might be, but few would be able to offer a definitive definition. Indeed, researchers, philosophers and educationalists rarely agree a definition, each having different perspectives. It would be arrogant, therefore, to suggest that this book would or could offer 'the' definition of creativity; the aim is to provide the reader with some current thoughts on what different people think creativity might be, and contextualise those ideas in relation to teaching and learning in primary science.

Children's insights into creativity

Throughout this book a constructivist approach has been used, eliciting the children's ideas on creativity. Constructivism advocates working from where the child is in their understanding, therefore acknowledging children's personal perceptions of the world. So, one of the main sources of thoughts on creativity comes from children themselves who offer remarkable insights into creativity and creative people. Each chapter of this book is based around a quotation from a primary aged child. Why? Because the children should be at the heart of creativity in primary science and because children themselves have a lot to teach us.

The opening quotation of this chapter provides a real insight into the purpose of creative education. The child understands the idea that developing creativity is a preparation for the future and that it provides the platform for lifelong creativity. Nurture creativity today and we will all reap the benefits tomorrow, either as individuals enjoying pastimes in science, as researchers, as inventors or captains of industry tapping into the creative capacity of a workforce. The challenge is to manage the formality of national curricula in an inspiring and creative way. We must, though, remember that creativity is not an add-on to the curriculum; it is, as the National Advisory Committee on Creativity and Culture in Education (NACCCE 1999: 101) stated, 'the general function of education'.

Children who receive an education that values and encourages creativity are more likely to become adults who have the capacity to be fascinated by ideas and experiences, enjoy challenges, to be spontaneous, be willing to take risks and able to look at things from a variety of perspectives. Society needs creative people. Most importantly, society needs people who can engage in science at different levels, from the researchers who develop new materials and products to a scientifically literate population that understands science and how scientists work, so that they can participate as active citizens in a democracy.

Creativity as a human right

Everyone has the capacity to be creative, some naturally and some needing support to recognise and realise their own creative potential. If children have the right to be creative in their personal and school life, they have the right to be creative and have their creativity developed in science. For this to happen, the school must establish a shared understanding of the nature of creativity in science, appreciate how to develop it in science and have, as a priority, the imperative that all children should have access to an environment that encourages and nourishes the creative spirit in this area of the curriculum.

On a deeper level, teachers must understand the nature of creativity and how to play their role in meeting that whole-school ethos. I have deliberately avoided suggesting a 'school policy' on creativity, since, if creativity is a basic human right (and indeed a basic human quality), then no school can flourish without naturally being a creative environment. However, it does take management of teaching and learning to ensure that creativity flourishes, not only for the pupils but also for those adults working in the school:

> All people have creative abilities and we all have them differently. When individuals find their creative strengths, it can have an enormous impact on self-esteem and on overall achievement. (NACCCE 1999: 6)

For many teachers, being able to explore his or her own professional creativity is what makes the teacher thrive in a school and enjoy his or her own job.

> I love to find different ways of engaging children in science. It's great when I think of an unusual starting point and the children are just so engaged. It's what keeps me going! (Teacher during in-service training)

It is essential that all those involved in a school, and in particular senior management, are committed to promoting creativity. The Office for Standards in Education indicates that:

> School leadership that is committed to promoting creativity is vital. Not only does this, in a sense, permit teachers and pupils to work creatively but also helps to ensure good practice is recognised, resourced and disseminated widely. (Ofsted 2003: 5)

Defining creativity

NACCCE created what could be seen as a seminal piece of work on creativity in their 1999 report *All Our Futures: Creativity, Culture and Education*. This report defined the nature and purpose of creative education and set out a range of practical recommendations. The following section draws on the contents of this report alongside the writing of key authors such as Sternberg (1999) and Boden (1992).

NACCCE (1999: 30) suggested that creativity is an: 'imaginative activity fashioned so as to produce outcomes that are both original and of value'.

NACCCE offers four key points related to this definition, suggesting that creativity relies on:

- thinking or behaving imaginatively;
- imaginative activity being purposeful;
- imaginative activity that generates something original; and
- the outcome being of value to the original objective.

Thinking and behaving imaginatively

> Imaginative activity is the process of generating something original: providing an alternative to the expected, the conventional, or the routine. (NACCCE 1999: 31)

The computer thesaurus suggests the following words related to 'imaginative': inventive; original; ingenious; inspired; artistic. Each of these words is presented in Table 1.1 with additional related words.

Table 1.1 Words defining 'imaginative'

Inventive	creative, imaginative, resourceful, ingenious, original
Original	unique, innovative, novel, inventive, creative, new, unusual, imaginative
Ingenious	clever, resourceful, original, inventive, creative, nifty, imaginative, inspired
Inspired	enthused, stimulated, stirred, moved, encouraged, motivated
Artistic	creative, imaginative, inventive, arty

The list offers a range of words associated with the idea of creativity, including being imaginative. The list suggests the vocabulary used to define what it means to be imaginative and the words provide excellent benchmarks for the kinds of attitudes and aptitudes that we should be encouraging in children.

Being imaginative involves 'mental play' – an interesting concept and one that is difficult for many teachers who are looking for right answers in science and who lack confidence in encouraging children to share ideas, pose questions and problems, often because they lack confidence in their own scientific understanding.

Mental play is rather like 'fooling around' with ideas, having 'fun' with alternatives and exploring different possibilities, where the individual looks at things from alternative perspectives and perceptions. Professor Lewis Minkin suggests that imaginative play is:

> a form of mental play – serious play directed towards some creative purpose . . . Creative 'play' – seeking to see the world afresh – is at times a fight against the fascination which familiar associations and directions of thought exert on us. Young people need to be encouraged to understand the importance of this kind of play. (NACCCE 1999: 31)

Nickerson in Sternberg (1999: 410) refers to this as 'intellectual playfulness – finding pleasure in playing with ideas'. Nickerson continues, suggesting that:

> It could be, too, that all children are curious and that whether they maintain their curiosity into adulthood depends to a large degree on the extent to which it is encouraged or inhibited in early life. (*ibid.*)

Imaginative activity being purposeful

Creativity does not just 'happen'. Each creative thought or action has a purpose behind it. Sometimes it is a spontaneous reaction to an observation, but more usually it has had a gestation period, where the person has thought, tried something out, refined, then finally come to an appropriate solution. Whenever someone is being creative they (invariably) are working towards producing something, an idea to share, a question to answer, a problem, an artefact, or indeed finding a way of working. The individual is working with a purpose and while those purposes might change, the creative endeavour nevertheless has a reason for being behind it.

Being original

This is an interesting concept in relation to science and children. Some theorists would suggest that for something to be original it has to be original to humankind. If we take this as being true, then creativity is limited to a minority of people who create something totally new to the human race, such as Darwin and his theory of evolution or Einstein and relativity. This begs the question, How can children be original in science when at times they are using the ideas developed by other people over time?

However, if we define creativity as being original to the individual, then this allows for everyone to have creative potential. In terms of primary science, two important categories are described in NACCCE (1999: 32):

> **Individual** – A person's work may be original in relation to their own previous work and output.
> **Relative** – It may be original in relation to their peer group – to other young people of the same age, for example.

In relation to educating young children, a working definition that allows for creativity to be original to the individual supports the idea that everyone is capable of original thoughts.

I know how your car works!

Consider the following scenario, a child being driven to nursery, who from the back seat of the car initiates the following conversation.

'I know how your car works!' he exclaimed.

'How?' asked the adult.

'Well, it's like this: you put your petrol into the wheels, they go round and the car moves!'

This is indeed an original thought. It is the first time the child has realised that he understands how a car works. At that moment in time, his thinking was the product of bringing together a range of experiences and ideas. While scientifically the idea is not correct, from the young child's perspective, the adult appears to put the petrol into the wheels, which are below the petrol cap. To the child, it is suddenly quite obvious how the car works. In fact, it is a revelation to the four-year-old, and is an example of constructivism in action, where the child is able to make limited sense of a phenomenon given his or her personal observations and knowledge at that particular time. Is it creative? Well, it is an original thought, using personal observations and knowledge of the environment as far as that child's experience goes, and the child has been purposeful in his thinking. The fact that it is not entirely correct should not diminish the creative sense the individual is making at that point in his life.

Must be of value in relation to the original objective

It follows that, if creativity has a purpose, then to be creative, the result must be related to the original objective. NACCCE suggests that:

> The outcome of imaginative activity can only be called creative if it is of value in relation to the task at hand. There are many possible judgements according to the area of activity: effective, useful, enjoyable, satisfying, valid, tenable. The criteria of value vary according to the field of activity in question. (1999: 33)

How might these criteria be translated in the classroom? What might creativity look like and can we recognise these individual features of creativity? NACCCE suggests that:

> In our view, creativity is possible in all areas of human activity and all young people and adults have creative capacities. Developing these capacities involves a balance between teaching skills and understanding, and promoting the freedom to innovate, and take risks. (1999: 35)

All children have the capacity to be creative. The following example tells the story of Bryn, a child with language difficulties.

The switch

The class were engaged in work on electricity and had reached the stage where they were exploring switches. The children were given a problem to solve and that was how to make their own switch for a circuit with a bulb in it. They were allowed to  choose from a wide range of materials. The children worked well and produced a range of switches, all of which the teacher had seen before, except for Bryn's. Bryn's switch involved a ramp, along which were strips of foil placed across the ramp, each one connected to the battery. To make the bulb light, a metal ball bearing was sent down the ramp, so that it passed over the strips of foil then onto the wooden ramp, then onto a strip of foil, then onto the ramp, thus making the bulb switch on and off.

Why was this a creative approach?

Bryn had a problem to tackle. His thinking was imaginative and quite different from the thinking of the rest of the class. His thinking and way of working was purposeful; his aim was to make the light switch on and off. The outcome of his thinking and behaviour was original in relation to his peers but also in terms of his own abilities. The switch was of value to the original problem. He had solved it in a novel way and had used his personal scientific knowledge of electricity and materials to do so.

Summary

This chapter has introduced creativity and outlined some of the definitions of creativity. The emphasis has been placed on the importance of both the teacher and the child being able to explore and develop their creative potential. Ideas relating to attempting to define creativity have been introduced, suggesting that a creative person thinks or behaves imaginatively in the process of trying to solve a problem or answer a question. The outcome of that process will be original to the person and relate to the original challenge. Most importantly creative experiences will help to shape who we are and, as the child in the opening quotation suggested, 'creativity helps you know more stuff about what you want to do when you're grown up'.

The following chapter begins to consider how creativity can be developed in the classroom. It begins by considering the idea that not only should creative activity have a purpose related to a specific goal, but that in science the development of creativity is a partnership, in which the children need to have a role. This suggests another dimension to the idea of purpose in creativity. That is, to develop children's appreciation of creativity and their own creative potential, so that they can deliberately work to develop their own creativity in science. It means that not only will children be engaged in creative behaviour but also in consciously developing their own creativity, thus becoming a partner with the teacher in realising their own creative potential.

ACTIVITY SUGGESTION: ICE SECRETS

Developing creativity

- To use and develop children's imagination.

- To encourage children to take risks in their thinking.

- To provide children with an opportunity to engage in 'mental play'.

Developing science

- To develop their ability to use science knowledge and understanding about changes in state and classification in a different and novel context.

- To develop children's ability to use evidence to draw conclusions.

Resources

ice columns

Language

ice   melting   freezing   evidence   habitat   animals   plants
conditions   classify   similarities   differences

Introduction

This activity could be used in a number of contexts, for example, rocks and soils, changes of state, or to develop children's understanding of using evidence in science to draw conclusions. For this activity the teacher will need to create columns of ice with evidence inside. These can be made using plastic tubes with lids. Inside the tube, place small plastic plants, animals, sample of soil, leaves etc. in water. Place the tube on its side in the freezer so everything does not move to the bottom and leave it until frozen. It is important to try to create a picture of the area that is consistent, for example, dinosaurs, large leaves, ferns or invertebrates, soils and plants.

Activity

Setting the context

Set the scene for the children, telling them that they are scientists working in the Antarctic and trying to find out as much about this area as possible. Their group of scientists has decided to drill into the ice so that they can take out a column of ice and analyse what is in the ice itself. The aim is to look for things in the ice that might give a clue as to what plants and animals lived in the Antarctic many years ago.

Analysing the ice column

Give each small group an ice column to analyse. Allow them to carefully scrape ice away to uncover their evidence. They should take notes on the evidence they find and then use the evidence to suggest what the environment was like when the evidence was frozen into the ice. They should use classification keys to find out what kind of animals or plants they have found.

Presenting their evidence

Children should be asked to communicate their findings to the rest of the class. Ask children to think of different ways. For example, depending on the age and ability of the children they could use:

PowerPoint   digital photographs   demonstrations   web page

Follow-up

Children could create their own ice columns. Before they do so, they will need to think about:

- What the environment was like.

- What kind of plants and animals were alive just before the ice developed.

- What the soil was like.

Once the ice columns have frozen, use them in the classroom. Give them to different groups to analyse and report their findings to the group that created the ice column.

CHAPTER 2

The creative child in science

 I let my mind run free and I'm quite daring. I like thinking the unthinkable.

(Margaret, age 8)

For children to be partners in the development of their own creativity, they need to develop an understanding of the concept of creativity and appreciate that they can take a role in developing and realising their own creative potential.

Children can develop an appreciation of creativity and produce their own set of criteria for creativity which they can then apply to their own work and development.

What is a creative person like?

The teacher and a mixed-age class of 9, 10 and 11-year-old children were involved in thinking about the idea of creativity. The children were invited to consider the word 'creativity' and what they thought a creative person was like. They were used to working with their 'talk partner' (their neighbour or the child he or she had been paired with to discuss ideas) and so they chatted to their partner about what special things made someone creative.

Their responses make interesting reading and provide excellent contributions to defining creativity. In fact, they are possibly more creative in their response than even the most well-written and established researchers and writers in the field!

Children's ideas of what is a creative person

Using a constructivist approach allowed the teacher to find out children's ideas of a creative person. The children were asked to draw a stick person in the middle of a page and write words and phrases around their 'stick figure'. Their ideas provided a starting point for discussion, allowing children to share and compare their ideas with the rest of the class. These responses can also provide an insight into what children recognise and value in themselves and other people.

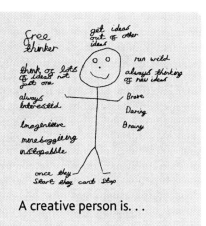

A creative person is. . .

How do children's ideas relate to creativity in science?

The ideas from the children provide interesting and powerful insights into how children's ideas relate to thinking and working scientifically and how their suggestions can be used to define someone who is creative. Throughout this book contributions from children will be used alongside those from a range of authors to help explain aspects of creativity. Children's ideas are important; they bring their own experiences and frameworks about themselves as learners to the school situation and we should access their thinking and make use of their ideas at every opportunity. In the following section, the ideas from the children are used to explore the potential characteristics of the creative child in primary science. The headings are taken from the statements provided by the children in the figures 'A creative person is . . .' and some of these are explored in relation to ideas about creativity.

'Let loose imagination'

This is a wonderful expression which suggests freedom to explore one's imagination and give free rein to ideas. This is essential in developing a classroom where creativity can flourish and also in recognising children who are engaged in creative thinking and working.

'Show thoughts'

This is a central tenet of primary science, since it is only through children being able to articulate their thinking that we can support them in moving forward in their learning. A confident, creative child will be able to share, indeed, often demand to share thoughts with others, because they are excited by the activity in which they are engaged and with their own ideas. The creative child, like scientists, will want to share ideas to help him or her clarify his or her thoughts by articulating them and literally hearing him or herself speak.

'Encouraging and joyful'

This is perhaps one of the most perceptive responses from the children, and one that many people would agree with: that a creative person is often a happy and lively person. In primary science the creative child will be someone who is enjoying science, is motivated, interested and lively when responding to ideas and activities. This does require the teacher to be aware that even those children who appear to be the most confident and engaged can still have their doubts.

Confidence in ideas

Andris, when writing a science fiction story, was very excited and lively, full of ideas, yet at the beginning he sat with a worried look on his face. Finally he put his hand up and the teacher went over and Andris said, 'I am not sure whether my ideas are good enough.' The teacher sat and listened to his ideas and then exclaimed, 'They are really wild, the most creative ideas I have read yet!' Andris grinned and replied 'Great!' then with confidence and enthusiasm went on to write a superb piece of work, which you can read in Chapter 10.

'Imagination run wild'

The science curriculum is not somewhere a teacher might necessarily think of as a place where imagination can be allowed to run wild. Science especially might be thought of as more staid; an area that relies on exact measurements and careful, logical thinking. Yet think of scientists throughout history. They have often had ideas that in their own time were wild and sometimes considered heresy. How liberating to be told that letting your imagination run wild is exactly what is wanted. How exciting for children to realise that they can and are expected to do so.

'Let your mind take over'

The creative child allows his or her mind to wander, to 'run wild' and take over, but in the classroom needs encouragement and the freedom to do this. It is important that the creative child is not only given permission to do this but that the child is not constrained by adult perceptions of the world.

A creative person is. . .

'Creative and daring'

This is an interesting statement from the children and one that suggests 'risk taking'. According to many writers in creativity (e.g. NACCCE 1999; Sternberg

1999), 'risk taking' is the hallmark of a creative person. Risk is usually synonymous with some kind of threat, placing oneself in jeopardy or being involved in something hazardous. In the context of creative primary science, 'risk' is related to thinking and working differently.

To a child this can be quite daring. Thinking of things and suggesting ideas which might be very different to those expected by the teacher or suggested by peers takes courage. It is the role of the teacher to encourage and support children in taking risks in their thinking and ways of working in science.

'Express imagination'

Primary science needs children to use their imagination. As a subject it frequently involves children accessing ideas and experiences that are counter-intuitive, such as equal and opposite forces, or that the sun only appears to move. Primary science invites children to imagine, for example, what blood looks like inside, how the solar system works and that gravity is pulling on us all. Children need to be able to take 'leaps of the imagination' as well as to express what they are thinking.

'Reach new heights'

The children who offered this perceptive statement realised that creative people shift their own boundaries and improve on their own personal best. That personal best in science might be ideas about a specific concept, a way of working or a strategy for finding solutions to a problem.

'Think the unthinkable'

This became one of the favourite sayings with the children engaged in this task – 'to think the unthinkable'. They revelled in the idea that they were being allowed, even encouraged, to think about things that they had not considered before. They liked the idea of being given permission and encouraged to work differently. The creative child may be the child who suggests something radical and takes everyone by surprise.

'New things'

How interesting that children should realise that creative people produce something new. NACCCE (1999) also came to this conclusion in their report, suggesting that one of the key elements of creativity is the ability to create something original. In the classroom this might manifest itself as a child suggesting a new way of working, creating a poem about seed dispersal or suggesting a novel approach to solving a problem linked to using equipment in an investigation.

'Get ideas out of other ideas . . . Once they start they can't stop. Unstoppable'

Children clearly realise that creative people have lots of different ideas. They also have some understanding that one idea can lead to another, and that one 'piggy-backs' on another idea. Creative children in science are children whose ideas flow, one after another and also those who thrive in a social situation where they can bounce ideas off other people in the classroom.

'Always interested'

The children, from their comments, appear to understand that creative people are motivated, have energy and are interested most of the time. Children who are creative in science will have a particular interest and often be the children who go home and search for more information, or try out ideas and activities from school.

'Mind-boggling'

Finally the suggestion that a creative person has ideas that are incredible, astonishing and amazing indicates how children perceive creative people. Creative people, as a group, include creative children, who also can have ideas that are mind-boggling!

Encouraging children to believe that they are creative

Obvious though it may seem, it is important that teachers and other adults working in the classroom encourage children to think and work creatively:

> Highly creative people in any field are often driven by a strong self-belief in their abilities in that field. Having a positive self-image as a creative person can be fundamental to developing creative performance. Many young people and adults do not think of themselves as creative and lack the confidence to take even the first step. (NACCCE 1999: 104)

NACCCE (1999) goes on to suggest that teachers should encourage children to believe that they are creative and allow them to explore their creativity during lessons. The children who shared their ideas about 'What is a creative person ...' were then encouraged, by their teacher, to be creative. The teacher asked the children to apply their own criteria and while they were working would ask the children:

- 'How mind-boggling is your idea?'
- 'Are you thinking the unthinkable?'
- 'Are you being creative and daring?'

Children acknowledging their own creative ability

I think I am creative because . . .

In another activity the children were asked to think about their own creative abilities. Interestingly the question was phrased in such a way that the children were not asked whether or not they were creative, but told that they were all creative in some way. They were then asked to share their thoughts on what was creative about themselves. Their responses were both varied and fascinating.

I think I am creative because...

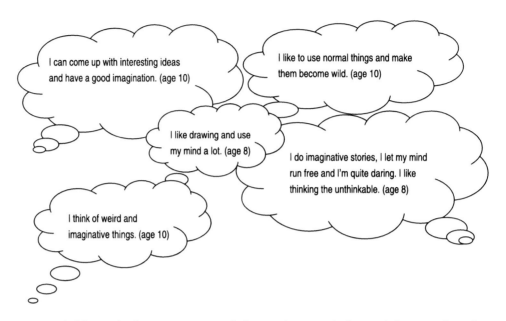

I can come up with interesting ideas and have a good imagination. (age 10)

I like to use normal things and make them become wild. (age 10)

I like drawing and use my mind a lot. (age 8)

I do imaginative stories, I let my mind run free and I'm quite daring. I like thinking the unthinkable. (age 8)

I think of weird and imaginative things. (age 10)

Most children do have a sense of themselves and their abilities. They have constructed this 'sense of self' from how friends, family, teachers and their peers in school see them. Considering the statements from the children, it becomes obvious that these children identify certain aspects in their own creativity. Children have different creative abilities, which should not be 'pigeonholed' into music, art, English or indeed science. While a child might consider him or herself gifted in art or English, they should also be encouraged to look upon those 'abilities' as tools which can be applied to many different aspects of life as well as the school curriculum. It would be foolish to suggest that every child could be at his or her most creative in science when they were a superb musician, artist or story writer, but many of the special abilities children possess can be transferred to and used in science, if the teacher recognises them and is prepared to support the child in exploiting those abilities. This is why providing the opportunity for children to consider the nature of creativity and how the nature of creativity relates to the way they think and work in science is so important. NACCCE suggests:

> Recognising and becoming more knowledgeable about the creative process can also foster creative development: teaching for creativity can assist young people in understanding what is involved in being creative and help them become more sensitive to their own creative process. (1999: 104)

Summary

This chapter has established that eliciting children's ideas on creativity is important and that children's ideas about creativity can be used to encourage children to be partners in developing their own creativity in science.

The next chapter considers issues relating to developing a classroom environment that is supportive of creative teaching and learning in science, and suggests ways in which the attributes the children have identified in this chapter can be developed.

ACTIVITY SUGGESTION: WHAT IS CREATIVITY?

Developing creativity

- To develop children's understanding of the concept of creativity.

- To encourage children to think about their own creative abilities.

Developing science

- To consider the idea that scientists are creative people.

- To think about what aspects of science are creative.

Resources

story or stories about scientists

Language

creative   creativity   imagination   different   curious   abilities

Introduction

Explain to children that the aim of the session is to think about creativity and that they will be thinking about some of the following:

- What they think creativity means.

- What kind of people are creative.

- How creative people think and act.

- Creativity and science.

- What it means to be creative in science.

Activity

A creative person is . . .

Give children a large piece of paper and ask them to draw a stick person in the centre. Explain to them they will be working with their 'talk partner' and discussing what they think creative people are like, for example, What do they think about? What do they do? How do they work? Before the children begin, use the whiteboard to model this approach and use children's suggestions. Then allow children to discuss their ideas with their talk partners and then write their ideas on their paper.

When children have completed this task, share and discuss their ideas. Ask them if they know any creative people and why they think that they are creative.

I am a creative person because . . .

In this activity ask children to write this opening statement on their individual whiteboards or a piece of paper and complete it. Tell them to think about the statements they placed on their page, from the first activity. When they are ready, ask children to share their ideas about themselves with the rest of the class. Children will often respond to what their friends write about themselves, by agreeing and offering examples of things that their friends have done that they think are creative.

How can I become a more creative person?

An important aspect of developing creativity in science is that children should understand that they can be a partner in developing their own creativity. Engage children in a discussion about how they think they might be able to help themselves become more creative (or indeed how the teacher might help them) in the science work as well as in other areas of the curriculum.

Follow-up

There are many stories about scientists which are accessible to children, both scientists from the past and contemporary scientists. Ask children to research a scientist and think about why that scientist was creative. Encourage children to use their own criteria for being creative. Children could research:

Aristotle   Albert Einstein   Marie Curie   Charles Drew

Helen Beatrix Potter   Diane Fossey   Jane Goodall   Elizabeth Garrett Anderson

Sir Humphry Davy   Stephen Hawking   Gregor Mendel   Susan Greenfield

Developing the creative classroom

 A creative person is not scared of trying something new every day.

(Mohammed, age 8)

Have you ever walked into a school and immediately thought, 'Yes! This place is buzzing'? How did you know? What signals or clues did the environment offer that made you think that school was somewhere in which children were eager learners, teachers were exciting and creativity was flourishing?

What do you think the ideal classroom environment for supporting creative science teaching and learning is like? There is no hard data to tell us what it should and should not be like, but common sense and an understanding of how children learn can be our guide to what kind of classroom environment would support creative teaching and learning in science. Could it be that it is a place where the creative person, whether it is the teacher or child, can 'try something new every day'?

If that is the case, the 'creative classroom' should be somewhere the teacher and children expect something new and interesting in science as a matter of course. Variety and interest would thus enhance the quality of the teaching and learning experience for both the teacher and the children. However, providing novel and interesting experiences is not sufficient. What must underpin all experiences in science, including those that are designed to develop creativity, is personal knowledge and understanding in science. Nickerson (1999) agrees that underpinning creativity is the need to develop the individual's personal knowledge and skills in science. Without this knowledge and understanding, how can children explore creatively ways of thinking and working in science?

The following example indicates the different elements, such as developing knowledge (such as forces), skills (using equipment) and attitudes (perseverance in problem solving) along with ways of working, sit within a classroom context which values and encourages personal creativity.

James the builder

James was four years old. One day he and the rest of the nursery class visited a building site as part of planned work to develop scientific ideas about materials and forces. They watched builders use cement, move bricks, push wheelbarrows and use different materials. On the next day, the children helped the teacher to create a building site in a corner of their room. There was scaffolding, a cement mixer made from a barrel, a crane to lift objects, bricks and hammers. There were even hard hats for the children. James arrived at nursery after the weekend, prepared to be a builder. He had insisted that his mother allow him to wear a check flannel builder's shirt, and so, along with his builder's belt and hard hat, James spent the week building. Each day he engaged in something different, working with forces when he built walls, learning about materials when he made cement, and pushes and pulls when he used the crane to lift objects from one place to another. He tried out ideas, solved problems and worked co-operatively with others.

Why was this a successful environment for science teaching and learning?

James and the other children used the role play area for several weeks to explore ideas about buildings, forces, materials, making things move and other ideas in science. The context of the building site offered rich and varied experiences and allowed James to be creative and try 'something new every day'.

The classroom environment for all children (but in particular early years) needs to encourage children to be creative. In this context the teacher, nursery nurses and assistants:

● offered the children real life experience;

● identified and planned to use what children knew and were able to do in science and provided activities to develop new experiences and areas of learning;

● brought the real life experiences into the classroom to simulate, as closely as they could, a building site;

● created a role play area with equipment and materials that children could use in a variety of ways, thus allowing them to be creative both as individuals and in small groups;

● offered opportunities for children to use their imaginations;

● allowed children to explore and share their ideas;

● celebrated creativity by providing time each day to share what children had been doing.

The ordered classroom

The creative classroom does not 'just happen'. It is more likely to emerge where, as Hay McBer suggests, effective teachers develop a classroom in which:

> A sense of order prevails in the classroom. Pupils feel safe and secure. Pupil management strategy is a means to an end: allowing maximum time for pupils to be focused on task, and thus maximising the learning opportunity. (2000: 1.2.8.)

Order and good classroom management can help to support an environment in which creativity flourishes. However, creativity needs to be an integral part of every aspect of teaching and learning and it also has to be explicit. NACCCE indicates that:

> Creativity can be 'taught'. Teachers can be creative in their own teaching; they can also promote the creative abilities of their pupils. The roles of teachers are to recognise young people's creative capacities; and to provide the particular conditions in which they can be realised. (1999: 11)

The creative classroom flourishes where there is a fundamental whole-school ethos that underpins the education of pupils. In such schools creativity is not an 'add-on' but the development of a relationship between adults and children (in the school) that aims to capitalise on teachers' and children's personal creativity. In primary science, creativity is more likely to exist where teachers are encouraged and challenged to develop their own creative ability and take professional risks in their approaches to teaching and learning. This requires a flexible and innovative approach to the science curriculum and is predicated on good leadership and management, and not a slavish response to national schemes.

The classroom environment

The classroom environment is three-dimensional. It requires attention to the *physical classroom* environment, which provides the backdrop and often the stimulus for thinking and working creatively in science. It also requires attention to the *social and emotional* environment, which encourages children to respect each other's ways of working and thinking. Finally the creative classroom requires attention to the *thinking* environment, where adults and children enjoy the challenge of sharing and exploring ideas and challenges.

The physical classroom environment

Primary teachers are adept at creating colourful, eye-catching displays; the display that supports creativity in science is not simply an attractive backdrop but is an integral part of the lessons and activities that children engage with.

Science displays that support thinking and working creatively would:

- contain children's ideas;
- include material to challenge ideas;
- offer questions and problems to think about;
- contain relevant scientific terminology;
- encourage children to try activities out, handle materials and make observations;
- allow children to register their responses and ideas;
- be fluid and change according to children's responses;
- change to provide different areas of interest and challenge.

Resources (which are dealt with in more detail in Chapter 6) are an important consideration in developing a classroom environment that supports creativity. Suffice to say that the range and quality of resources children have access to is crucial and that access needs to be based on the premise that children should be responsible for choosing, using and returning resources.

Equally important is the need for organisation, as Duffy indicates:

The way in which we organize and use the available space inside and out is crucial to creating opportunities for children to express their creativity . . . It is frustrating for children and adults if they are delayed and possibly distracted by being unable to find a resource or piece of equipment at a crucial moment. (1998: 105)

The nature of primary science demands that children become independent in their use and choice of resources. Fundamental to primary science is the requirement that teachers organise their classroom to facilitate children's independence. What often happens is that very young children work in an environment that maintains such a climate of organisation and expectation. Then as children move through the primary years, this independence is taken from them because the way in which the science curriculum and management of lessons is constructed denies children autonomy. Many schools need to rethink their approach, to meet not only the requirements of primary science but also the needs of children as emerging, independent and creative people in science.

The social and emotional environment

The social and emotional environment where creativity flourishes is one where children feel safe to express and try out their ideas. In science this can be difficult since children might have thoughts that are different from other people, which means that they might be subject to ridicule. Sharing ideas for some children is a risk. What will others think of their suggestions? Are they wrong? Will someone laugh or will their ideas just be ignored? Children asked to think about the characteristics of a creative person offered a range of ideas, some of which refer to the emotional and social aspects of creativity, such as being confident, helping others, being open to other ideas and developing independence. All these characteristics children see as important in a creative person. Their ideas are valid and provide the basis for the teacher to consider whether or not the classroom's social and emotional environment in science supports these.

In making sense of creativity, children have their own ideas of those aspects that are important to them in ensuring that they feel confident to be creative, try out new things, explore ideas and take risks in science. Below are some thoughts expressed by children, and they help to suggest what kind of support children require.

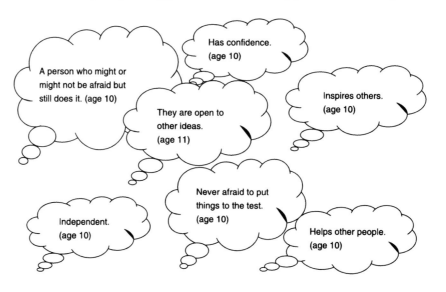

Feldman (1999: 176) identifies the importance of 'interpersonal, social and educational relationships' indicating that the development of creativity is a complex mix of these aspects. If children are correct in their assumptions as to the characteristics of a creative person, and no research so far contradicts them, then the emotional and social environment in which primary science is taught should encourage children to:

- listen to each other;
- respect each other's ideas;
- be independent;
- support and help each other;
- take risks;
- learn from mistakes;
- feel that they can inspire others and be inspired by their peers.

Talking about these issues, agreeing rules for working together and helping children to realise that they can learn from each other should be central to primary science and, in being so, will support creativity in primary science.

The thinking environment

The creative environment is a 'thinking environment' where the expectation is to:

- think for yourself;
- join in thinking;
- listen to the ideas (thinking) of others;
- be prepared to think differently;
- take risks in thinking.

When teaching primary science, the classroom environment needs to be conducive to thinking; it should be non-threatening and respectful of the child yet demand that individuals participate, and it should motivate them to do so. Self-esteem may be a key factor. When children feel that their ideas have currency and are valued, they are more likely to participate. Yet this takes time and the continued effort of the teacher to build a relationship of trust: a relationship that is not compromised by low expectations of the children's abilities nor that underestimates and undermines their thinking and creative potential.

Wallace and Louden suggest that in some cases:

> Students' ideas, beliefs and expectations about teaching and learning have been conditioned by particular kinds of teaching and assessment practices that promote dependency.
> (2002: 242)

Their reference, which relates to secondary education, has some resonance in primary situations. National curricula in science are often accompanied by prescriptive schemes and assessment systems that lead teachers to teach to the test. These approaches can result in a classroom environment where children are not encouraged to become independent thinkers, since teachers sometimes assume this approach to be time-consuming and less productive. Time is often seen as the enemy of creativity in the classroom, teachers often citing 'time' as being in short supply. The purpose of primary science should be to help develop the scientifically literate individuals of the future. These future scientifically literate generations must be able to engage in critical thinking and be confident to take risks. Good primary science demands that children think for themselves. This is not a luxury – it is an essential criterion for successful teaching and learning. The *thinking* environment should therefore be characterised by opportunities for the children to have time to engage in critical reflection, so that a gestation period might help children to form their ideas.

An environment of high expectations

Setting high expectations is important to science as for all forms of teaching and learning, and certainly important to creativity. NACCCE (1999: 29) suggests that high expectations are central to developing creativity and that the consequences of not setting them will be: 'frustration or waste of creative capacities in our schools'. High expectations are not just about the content of science and reaching targetted levels but about developing children as partners in their own learning, who understand the creative process and can share some of the responsibility for their own learning.

NACCCE suggests that:

> Encouraging, monitoring, reflecting upon their own performance and progress, and thinking about their own thinking – metacognition – can enhance young people's control over their creative activity and the development of their best practice. In these ways the aim is to encourage the development of the self-directed learner. Teaching for creativity encourages a sense of responsibility for learning. (1999: 106)

McBer (2000) suggests that 'high expectations' are developed by:

- communicating high expectations to pupils;
- setting expectations that are appropriate to the individual;
- being consistent;
- motivating pupils to achieve;
- encouraging pupils to take some of the responsibility for their own learning;
- making use of pupils' own ideas and experiences both in the classroom and outside.

Summary

An environment that encourages creativity in science should be a safe and supportive environment but it should also be an adventurous one, where, as suggested at the beginning of this chapter, 'A creative person is not scared of trying something new every day.'

The next chapter explores the idea of a 'creative science cycle' as an aide to thinking about planning for creative science opportunities and developing children's creative capacities.

ACTIVITY SUGGESTION: YUKKY GOO

Developing creativity

- To use and develop children's imagination.

- To encourage children to take risks in their thinking and activity.

- To offer children an opportunity to explore language linked to experiences using the senses.

Developing science

- To think about the properties of a material.

- To ask questions about how the property of a material can be changed and try out ideas.

Resources

mixing bowl   cornflour   spoon   water   cup   apron

Language

cornflour   properties   material   change reversible

irreversible   liquid   solid

Introduction

Science lesson planning should include surprises where children's experiences and ideas are challenged. In this activity the children make their own 'Yukky Goo' by following a simple set of instructions (to make a cornflour and water mixture). It is important that the children make this substance since as they follow the recipe they will already be forming ideas about how the material will behave. The final mixture behaves differently depending on how it is handled. If the mixture is allowed to flow through the fingers then it acts like a liquid, but if the mixture is squeezed and rolled it behaves like a solid.

The science behind this relies on an understanding of molecules; if the mixture is squeezed the water molecules are forced to rub against each other causing friction and the mixture behaves like a solid. When the pressure is taken off and it is allowed to flow freely then the molecules move apart and it flows like a liquid.

Activity

Challenge the children to change the mixture

Ask the children to think about what would happen if they tried to change the mixture and what they would do? For example, they might suggest:

- Put more water into the mixture.

- Put more cornflour in the mixture.

- Try a different kind of flour.

- Use warm instead of cold water.

Compare Yukky Goo with other materials

Provide children with a collection of other interesting materials that they can mould and change. Ask children to record their observations in relation to similarities and differences.

Follow-up

Collect children's comments about the Yukky Goo and place them onto the class 'Exploration Table' where they can read what others have said as well as continue to explore the substance. Ask children to create their own new scientific words to describe the properties of the Yukky Goo thus allowing them to play creatively with language.

The creative science cycle

 I can come up with interesting ideas and have a good imagination; I can make things from nothing.

(Tracey, age 10)

In developing a model for creative science, the central feature is the partnership between the teacher and the children where both understand and work towards being creative in science. This requires the teacher to engage the children in a dialogue about how to think and work creatively and sets a range of expectations relating to how the teacher and children will work when engaged in thinking and working scientifically. This has implications which are encapsulated in the following statement:

> I feel that communicating to the children that they are expected to be creative almost gives them licence to free their imaginations and tackle school work in a way that normally wouldn't occur to them. (Ruth Tait-Bridges, Teacher)

Here the teacher is acting as a positive role model for the children and other teachers by expressing her personal philosophy that the teacher must communicate his or her expectations that the children should 'work in a way that normally wouldn't occur to them'. To accomplish this the teacher needs to model an approach and scaffold alternative ways so that children can have success in thinking the unthinkable, take risks in sharing ideas that are different, consider a range of ideas and be prepared to consider alternatives offered by other children. Figure 4.1 illustrates a possible model for this approach and demonstrates how children's ideas about the characteristics of a creative person fit into the model.

To many people, the model may look familiar; in fact, it is not too dissimilar to approaches to planning in primary science. That is because it is based on planning in primary science. However, there is a difference, and that is the context; the cycle is set against a background where teaching and learning creatively have a higher profile and are included as an explicit element of planning. Where creativity has such a profile, the demands made of children in relation to how they approach their science are different.

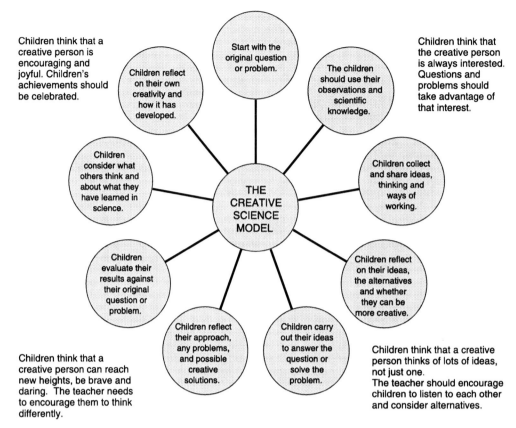

Figure 4.1 The Creative Science Model

Asking questions and suggesting problems in science

Feasey suggests that:

> Science depends on questions. It is the way in which human knowledge is taken forward. Should scientists ever stop asking questions then the consequences are unimaginable, progress and understanding of the world would remain static. (in Sherrington 1998: 156)

Children are the scientists, they ask questions because, as Feasey indicates, 'it is how they make sense of the world and take their personal knowledge forward' (*ibid.*). Creativity in primary science has at its centre the teacher as an effective questioner who acts as a role model; someone who encourages children to be curious, notice detail and asks not just any question, but questions that are deliberately challenging.

While the planning model suggests that the various elements are part of a whole activity, it is important that the teacher uses every opportunity to develop children's creativity in all aspects of science.

The following example is taken based on a set of books by Feasey, Goldsworthy, Phipps and Stringer (2003) which suggest that science should also be taught outside formal, timetabled lessons, for example, a six or ten-minute science session at any point in the school week. The aim of a six to ten-minute science session is for the teacher to take the opportunity to show the children something that is 'awesome', that challenges their notion of what might happen or sparks off interest and curiosity. During the session, the formal science curriculum is set aside to allow a 'free flow' of ideas and questions to help develop children's innate curiosity and imaginative thinking – in other words, creativity.

Floating cola cans

The teacher took into the classroom two cans of cola, one diet and one ordinary. She asked the children to think about what would happen if she placed both cans, unopened, into a tank of water.

The children, working with their 'talk partner', discussed their ideas and then suggested what would happen. Their ideas varied from the diet drink floating and the other sinking, the cans flipping over in the water, to both cans sinking.

When placed in the water, both cans floated but the diet drink floated higher than the other ordinary can of cola.

There was a buzz of astonishment in the classroom as they watched the cans bobbing in the water at different levels. Usually the diet cola floats higher than the normal cola. The children were asked to think about why one floated higher than the other. Here are some of their ideas.

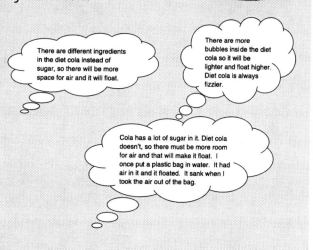

There are different ingredients in the diet cola instead of sugar, so there will be more space for air and it will float.

There are more bubbles inside the diet cola so it will be lighter and float higher. Diet cola is always fizzier.

Cola has a lot of sugar in it. Diet cola doesn't, so there must be more room for air and that will make it float. I once put a plastic bag in water. It had air in it and it floated. It sank when I took the air out of the bag.

The children were asked to think about what other things they could test and why they would want to test them. Their ideas included:

- Using smaller cans, to see if size affects how they float.

- Comparing bottles of diet and ordinary cola.

- Putting still drinks like cans of orange juice in the water.

- Opening the cans to see if it makes any difference if the fizz is taken out.

- Pouring the cola in plastic cups with lids on to see what happens.

Later in the week the children were given the opportunity to test out their ideas.

Why was this a creative episode?

The teacher took into the classroom something that was novel and of immediate interest to the children and something that would challenge children's expectations. She encouraged the children to draw upon their personal knowledge and some children reached into their own everyday experience, while others drew upon their scientific understanding. The children were intrigued by what happened and quickly began to offer imaginative suggestions about what they could do next. The teacher was not worried about meeting curriculum outcomes but more concerned with encouraging children to explore ideas without the constraints of expecting the correct scientific response:

You really do occasionally have to loosen the reins, as a teacher, so that you can allow the pupils to show you what they can really do and think about when given the right opportunities. (Bukky Yusuf, Teacher and science consultant)

The creative teacher is able to manage pupil learning in such a way that he or she engineers experiences where the children are able to lead the learning. This can be achieved by enabling children to suggest their own questions and consider problems in which they, with the support from the teacher, are challenged to find their own solutions. Where children ask their own questions and pose their own problems there is a sense of ownership and motivation to answer them. Questions and problems in science should avoid being closed but be open and therefore not directed to only one solution, which by its very nature would then preclude creative approaches to their solution. De Boo reminds us about the difficulty of setting realistic and appropriate problems in science:

> Problems in real life are likely to be multi-faceted with several options, any one of which may present further problems. In these situations we learn to compromise and choose the 'best fit' for the circumstances. Many of the problems children meet in school are abstracted from reality, with one 'right answer'. (1999: 134)

Collecting and sharing ideas and thinking about ways of working

When children are faced with questions and problems to answer in science, they need to be encouraged to draw upon personal scientific knowledge and everyday experience. A crucial element in working creatively in science is the opportunity for children to engage in discourse with both adults and their peers.

Harlen reflects that:

> The presence of one or more other people is essential in these cases, not only to legitimate thinking aloud but for offering the occasional comment or question for clarification which has the effect of provoking reflection on what we think as we express it. The same things happen with young children though often less tidily, since the reflection is going on in several minds at the same time. (2000: 108)

Thinking through ideas relating to the original question or a problem in science should be a collaborative process. Children are more likely to be creative in their responses when they are working with others and able to share ideas with other members of the group. In Chapter 2 the children indicated that 'getting ideas out of other ideas' is an important aspect of creativity. Children, like adults, need other people to bounce ideas off and to spark new ideas. This communal thinking allows children to 'risk take' with suggestions. Interestingly, children often get carried away with their ideas, becoming more and more excited and sometimes more extreme with suggestions. This is part of the process of exploring the parameters of the problem and its possible solutions.

For some children this will require making a compromise when the time comes to make a decision about which route to take, and it might require subtle teacher intervention to help a group come to an agreement on what is realistic. This means that sometimes children will take a circuitous route filled with wonderfully imaginative ideas, but this is part of the creative process – thinking the unthinkable and then making it happen.

Carrying out ideas and problem solving

Much problem solving requires original thinking. Sternberg (1999: 394) suggests that 'the relationship between creativity and problem solving is very close', while Guildford (1975) offers ideas about what constitutes elements of creative problem solving. They include the following:

- the ability to recognise problems;
- being able to offer a number of ideas in relation to solving a problem;
- the ability to change approaches to solving a particular problem;
- the originality of ideas used to solve the problem.

In early years education, children explore through play and, if the contexts and materials are carefully chosen, this can lead children to encounter problems to solve and questions to ask. Siraj-Blatchford and MacLeod-Brudenell quote Craft (1997: 53) who suggests that:

> At the core of science is the need for children to think creatively: to experiment, to be open to possibility, to take risks, to be prepared to combine old ways of seeing with new ones, to be prepared to look at a situation or problem in different ways, to seek innovation, to be resourceful. (1999: 34)

Children must be allowed to solve a range of problems. There are, as De Boo (1999) suggests, two different kinds of problems. The first is those problems that are intellectual, requiring thinking, and secondly those problems that are mechanistic in nature (those problems that are more physical than cognitively challenging).

In science it is intellectual problems that demand that children engage in a range of cognitive processes which include:

- Defining the problem.
- Considering prior experience and knowledge, i.e. 'What do I already know about this kind of problem?'
- Asking 'Is there just one way of solving this problem or does someone have another idea?'
- Asking 'Do we need help with our problem?' (Children need to develop the ability to reflect and realise that they are unable at that point to continue forward without some assistance.)

> The value of creative thinkers is not only that they solve problems we know we have, but that they find problems we hadn't imagined and lead us on to new horizons. More opportunities should be given to young people to sense and define problems for themselves, as well as identifying solutions to given problems. More opportunities should be given to the generation of ideas: looking at the world in different ways and playing with different possibilities and alternative solutions. Familiarity with a wide range of problem-solving activities can lead to greater competence in seeing underlying patterns and analogies. (NACCCE 1999: 37)

Evaluating against original question or problem

Central to the creative science cycle is the notion of children being involved as reflective learners. Even young children can engage in thinking about their own thinking. Gardner (1993: 106) suggests that: 'Children not only think better as they mature; they also become capable of thinking about their own mental processes.'

Here Gardner is alluding to children developing metacognitive skills, that is, being able to think about their own thinking; for example, being able to suggest what made them think about something, or where they got their ideas from. De Boo (1999) cites Fisher (1990: 55) who states that:

> Metacognitive thinking is objective awareness of our own thinking and usually develops later, but this thinking can be encouraged if children are given opportunities and stimuli.

Thinking about our own thinking and other people's thinking is challenging. It is also risky, as De Boo suggests:

> Critical thinking or reflective thinking is concerned with our ability to assess the effectiveness of our thinking ... Thinking critically is not easy: our cherished theories can be proved 'wrong' and this can damage our self-esteem or require readjustments in our behaviour – an uncomfortable process. (1999: 64)

Critical thinking underpins creativity, as does risk taking. Sharing ideas that might be different and exploring those ideas might be uncomfortable and risky in terms of our own self-esteem. Science demands these personal dispositions. Primary science needs to come to terms with them and develop them as an integral part of teaching and learning. Hence the inclusion in the Creative Science Model (Figure 4.1) of the children's statements about 'reaching new heights' and being 'brave' and 'daring'. These are the attributes that children consider to be key to a creative person. They are laudable and in keeping with research and thinking by adults about creativity. Children are astute; they can reflect on learning; and their voices need to be heard and included in their teacher's thinking and approaches to primary science.

In terms of evaluation, the creative science cycle includes encouraging children to reflect on their own development as creative individuals. It may come as a surprise to some to find that children can reflect on their own development and that of others.

How might this be achieved in the classroom? Effective and sympathetic questioning is at the heart of supporting children in reflecting on their own creativity.

- What do you think was the most creative thing you have done?

- What do you think was your best idea today and why?

- We listened to lots of people today. Whose ideas did you think were really interesting? Why?

- Creative people have to persevere – keep on trying, even if something goes wrong. Who thinks that they had to persevere today? Why?

Celebrate creativity

Finally, either during or towards the end of the process, we must not forget to celebrate success, or as the children suggest, 'be encouraging and joyful'. Children respond to the teacher who gets excited about their ideas or their successes and provides positive feedback. Equally, when allowed to do so, children can offer equally enthusiastic responses to their friends' contributions to the process.

Helping children to feel a sense of accomplishment and to help children to find out what they are good at and how that contributes to the whole process is an important aspect of developing a child's creativity.

Magnets

A class of six and seven-year-olds were given a selection of magnets and different materials. They were told to find out as much about the magnets as they could and also to think about what they would like to find out about them.

The children spent time exploring with the magnets, working with a partner, and at the end of the time allocated the teacher collected what they had found out and scribed their ideas into a class book on magnets. The pages entitled 'What we know about magnets' included the following ideas.

The teacher engaged children in discussion about the magnets, introducing new language such as 'magnetic', 'repel', 'attract'. She then asked children, working with their talk partner, to think about 'really interesting' questions about magnets that they would like to find the answers to.

The challenge to think of 'really interesting' questions was discussed and the children rose to the occasion and decided what they wanted to know about. The questions were logged in a class book of questions and the children then worked in small groups to answer those questions through exploration and investigation.

There are different kinds of magnets.

Magnets pick up metal things.

Magnets can stick together.

Magnets push each other away.

Some magnets are very strong.

Some magnets don't work very well.

When the children had sufficient understanding of magnets, they were then given the problem of creating a magnetic game for younger children. This challenge posed many questions and children used their understanding of magnets and magnetic materials to develop very creative games. In the process they encountered a range of different problems, setbacks and disappointments when an idea did not work. Determination, perseverance and looking for alternative ways around their problems was explicitly encouraged and praised, and the teacher deliberately used the language of creativity when supporting children in their task.

Why was this a creative teaching and learning approach?

The teacher offered children experiences from which they could learn something and then at a later point draw upon their new knowledge. She allowed them to be in charge of their own learning by offering them an activity that was not dominated by worksheets, but instead, an activity that allowed them to bypass what they already knew and move on to find out new things about the magnets. She then challenged them to ask further questions and consider how they would answer their questions. In applying their knowledge to making the magnetic game, children were challenged to offer original ideas, as they developed those ideas they had to overcome problems and sometimes their own inadequacies. At all points, the teacher made demands on the children's ability to evaluate their approach and final product, in relation to the original problem, through effective and well-timed questions.

Their success was celebrated by talking about the different games, what was creative about them and why, with children congratulating each other on their achievements. At a later date the younger children in the school played the games with great enthusiasm which was another celebration of the children's success.

Summary

This chapter has offered a model for developing creativity in science that links to models already in use for primary science by teachers. Creativity must not be seen as an 'add-on' but integral to primary science, part of the normal teaching and learning process. It is important for children to be part of a partnership in developing their own creativity. This means that we need to encourage children to think about their own abilities. The quotation from a child at the beginning of the chapter shows that, when asked, a child can reflect on what is special about themselves. The challenge for the teacher is to help them to use and develop it.

In the next chapter, issues are explored related to planning science lessons that are creative and encourage children to be creative.

ACTIVITY SUGGESTION: TEDDY'S NEW CURTAINS

Developing creativity

- To develop problem-solving abilities.

- To engage children in a creative context.

- To encourage children to be creative in their questioning.

Developing science

- To develop children's use of computer sensors to solve a science-based problem.

- To make systematic observations and measurements.

Resources

computer light sensors   assorted fabrics   washing powder   washing line

Language

light   sensor   measure   fabric   transparent   translucent
opaque   fair   results   conclusion   table   graph

Introduction

Young children (for example, six and seven-year-olds) can use computer sensors to carry out simple investigations. Prior to using light sensors, children will need the opportunity to explore using the sensors to find out how they work and how to interpret the reading on the computer. This will require some teacher input and can be carried out using an interactive whiteboard to teach how to use the sensors. Then the children should be allowed to explore using the sensors. Provide the children with a story context for their investigation, for example, Teddy is having his bedroom redecorated and would like some new curtains. He would like his curtains to:

- be colourful;

- be easy to wash and quick drying;

- allow some light to come through so that he knows when it is morning but not too much light.

Activity

Provide children with a range of fabrics and ask them to think about how to plan and design a test to find out which curtains are best. Allow children to work in groups of three and discuss their plans before sharing them with the teacher and/or the rest of the class. Ask children to think about:

● What do they already know that would help them to plan their investigation?

● Have they shared ideas with each other?

● Did they listen to each other and use the best ideas to plan their test?

● What different and interesting ways of working did people in the group suggest?

While they are carrying out their investigation, encourage children to think about any problems they experience and work together to solve them. Once the investigation has been completed, the children should communicate their investigation and results to the rest of the class. At this point children should be encouraged to:

● Reflect on their activity – did it work?

● Think about how well the group worked and any interesting ideas.

● Congratulate the group on their accomplishments.

Follow-up

One of the other questions posed was 'Which curtains are easy to wash and dry?' The children could test their best fabrics to find out which one washes and dries best. At the end of the activity, ask children to think of an interesting way to tell Teddy about their activity and results. They might think about:

a letter   a video   photographs   label for the fabric

a washing line with fabrics and captions pegged on

Planning for a creative science lesson

 Are we still being creative?

(Christopher, age 8)

Constraints to planning for creativity in science

A small-scale research project on creativity in science was carried out by myself (Feasey 2004). One hundred primary teachers were asked the question, 'What do you think are the constraints for teaching and learning creatively in the classroom?' The majority of responses focused on increase in paperwork linked to school inspection and the high level of planning for subjects across the curriculum. Many teachers stated that they felt exhausted and unable to find the time and energy to be creative.

Teachers also suggested that the amount of content required in terms of curriculum coverage also meant that there was not enough time to allow children the opportunity to be creative in the classroom. Teachers also shared concerns that if they taught creatively it would jeopardise school results in national tests and school positions in performance tables. All the issues raised by teachers are real in relation to the day-to-day routine of schools and indicate the dilemmas faced by teachers. However, they uncover basic misconceptions about the nature of creativity. Creativity is not an add-on to the curriculum but an integral part of thinking and planning for teaching and learning episodes. Creativity requires that teachers are open to different possibilities and also to appreciate that developing creativity is not an option to be disregarded but that, as professionals, we have a duty to be creative and develop creativity in children. Some teachers indicated that it helped them to think about the fundamental reasons and ideals that brought them into the teaching profession in the first place:

> I came into teaching because I enjoyed being creative and trying to find the best approaches for the children. Over the years I have lost that and the enjoyment of teaching, but now I know that I have to reclaim that. After all, I am the only one who can do it. (Teacher on an in-service course)

The role of senior management in supporting creativity in science

Planning for creativity requires a whole-school approach. NACCCE (1999) confirms this and the Qualifications Curriculum and Assessment (QCA) organisation identifies the following as central to developing creativity across the curriculum (see website www.ncaction.org). It suggests that senior management must:

- value creativity in a school;
- encourage professional learning and development;
- build partnerships with external organisations, e.g. industry, to enrich learning;
- provide opportunities for pupils to work with creative people;
- provide a stimulating physical environment;
- manage time effectively;
- celebrate pupils' creativity.

Against this background, the role of the teacher is to:

- set a clear purpose for pupils' work;
- be clear about freedoms and constraints;
- fire pupils' imagination through other learning experiences;
- give pupils opportunities to work together.

Ofsted suggests that:

Creative work also often needs unbroken time to develop. Primary schools which maintained sufficient flexibility in their timetables for lessons to be blocked or extended to accommodate planned events or just to provide more time for creative activities, found it easier to enable this kind of development. (2003: 12)

Planning for creativity

Since creativity is often linked to spontaneity and more bohemian approaches to life, it might feel counter-intuitive to suggest that creativity is more likely to flourish in environments where clear frameworks are set and lesson planning is structured and sits within the context of carefully negotiated and structured whole-school planning.

The important word here is 'framework' – whole-school and individual lesson plans should offer a framework that is both clear and structured but flexible enough to respond to the needs of the teacher and the pupils.

At the macro level, schools need to consider and plan for developing an environment and culture that allows creativity to flourish in both its staff and pupils. At the micro level of the classroom, the teacher needs to be aware of the needs and potential of the individual children in the classroom and plan to support and tap that potential, whatever it might be. In an ideal world we should not need to discuss creativity in science, as it should be fundamental to teaching and learning so that no child should need to ask, 'Are we still being creative?' It should be second nature to teachers and children.

Planning for approaches to learning and creativity in science

McBer (2000) indicates that effective teachers employ a range of strategies to support learning in the classroom. This is a basic tenet of teaching and learning.

The creative teacher offers rich experiences to encourage creativity, by actively seeking to capitalise on the full range of learning styles across science teaching.

The creative teacher appreciates that some children require learning contexts that are more frequently biased towards one way of learning than others. Using a multi-sensory approach across science teaching, where the range of activities is drawn from the different areas, is important. Table 5.1 can be used as a check against which to reflect on the extent of the range used in personal teaching.

Table 5.1 Activities linked to multi-sensory approaches to learning

Visual	Aural	Kinaesthetic
Classroom displays	Music	Making things
Concept maps/cartoons	Sound games	Practical hands-on
Visualisation	Voice	Drama/role play
Using real objects	Discussion/debate	Sorting activities
Pictures/images	Drama/role play	Use of actions
Drama/mime	Tape recorder	Games
Interactive whiteboards	Video	3D models
Computer microscopes	Phonetic – clapping out sounds	Puppets
Visual games	Spoken word books/computer	
Text	Computer software	
Diagrams	Demonstrations	
Graphs/tables	Puppets	
Simulations	Interactive whiteboard	
Puppets	Talk partners	
Video		

Ice hands

Children were shown a box with a surprise in it: the box contained ice hands. (Visual)

They were challenged to ask questions to help them work out the contents of the box. (Aural)

Children were then given ice hands to explore and talk about in groups of three. (Visual, kinaesthetic, aural)

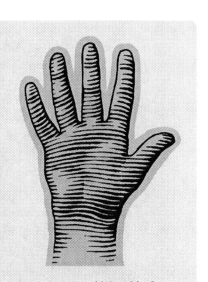

Children drew an ice hand and wrote questions around the ice hand. (Visual)

Children shared their questions with the rest of the class. (Aural)

Observing the children during this lesson, all children enjoyed the visual 'shock' of seeing ice hands and revelled in being able to handle them. All the children engaged with the sharing of ideas but there were at least eight children who really enjoyed sharing ideas. Four children were limited in their participation and required more support and encouragement, which was the norm for them. The latter group, when physically handling the ice hands, offered interesting and creative ideas and comments. They, more than other children in the class, needed practical experience to help initiate response from them.

Why was this a creative lesson?

This lesson was well planned with sound outcomes in relation to different elements of primary science, as illustrated in Table 5.2. The teacher herself reflected on the lesson and gave her reasons why the lesson was creative.

Table 5.2   Analysis of creative lesson

Element of lesson	Science skills	Science knowledge	Creativity
Presentation of ice hands as a surprise – children challenged to ask questions.	Asking questions.	Using personal knowledge to reflect on questions asked by others and ask new questions.	Showing interest and excitement. Willing to persevere with a range of questions, and be imaginative with questions.
Exploring ice hands.	Observation. Handling materials. Asking questions. Working together sharing ice hands.	Knowledge of changes in state. Using knowledge and scientific vocabulary to describe observations, e.g. some parts of the hands were transparent.	Sharing ideas and allowing ideas to flow. Being curious about different features of the ice hand. Allowing own thinking to explore different ideas.
Asking questions about the ice hand.	Observation. Handling materials. Asking questions. Asking questions with different question stems, e.g. Why? What if? Which?	Using knowledge to ask questions about melting, freezing, how the ice hand was made.	Asking a range of questions and rising to the challenge to ask different questions to extend their own knowledge. Being curious. Suggesting what might happen or what they could do with the ice hands.
Celebrating creativity.	Reviewing ideas offered by children.	Considering which questions and ideas were new and interesting.	Reflecting on discussion and who they thought had made interesting and creative contributions and why.

I felt that the 'ice hands' activity was extremely useful, not only as a catalyst for all sorts of creative thinking, but also as a means for children with a variety of learning styles to access 'tricky' concepts in science. (Ruth Tait-Bridges, Teacher)

Time management

Creative science lessons (as any good science lesson) need to be a fine balance between a brisk pace and ensuring that children are allowed thinking time, for critical reflection. Pupils need to be aware of time allocations as they progress through their primary years. There are many simple devices that can assist the teacher in letting children know how much time they have available for an activity. They include:

- stop watches;
- kitchen timers with alarms;
- sand timer;
- piece of music;
- counting down at regular intervals.

Simple timekeeping devices are important to keep children on task and to develop children's responsibility to manage their own learning. After all, there are only so many hours in a school day and there is no reason why children should not have to think and work creatively within some time constraints, provided that they do not inhibit ideas and pressurise those children who require more time to complete activities. Many pupils enjoy working against time constraints, although some find this intimidating unless supported.

NACCCE reminds us that the creative process requires time to 'stand back in quiet reflection' and suggests that teachers who aim to teach for creativity:

> Convey an appreciation of the phases in creative activity and the importance of time, including the ways in which time away from a problem may facilitate its solution. (1999: 105)

A science lesson that supports creativity is one that has pace; where the time in the lesson is well managed, the lesson has a clear structure and the children understand the purpose of the lesson. The transitions from one part of the lesson to another should be appropriate, well managed and explained to the children, so that they understand where they are going in the overall 'map' of the lesson. A well-managed lesson ensures that what is expected of the children is achievable within the limitations of the time available.

In contrast to the idea of briskness of pace is the concept of offering children time for reflection. Creativity requires a gestation period. Making time for children to think, reflect on their own ideas and those of other people is important. Equally it is important for children to be given time to explore alternatives as well as to take time out from the lesson to have a 'rest' from thinking and be able to return to the problem or question at their leisure. Sometimes this manifests itself in allowing children to go home and think about a problem, research information and even try out their own ideas. It can also be as simple as allowing children time to finish their conversations with peers by indicating to children that you would like them to finish their important talk in about three minutes. This allows children to come to a natural end point in their discussions rather than having the teacher say 'Stop now', cutting short their conversation and ideas, as well as frustrating children because they have not finished discussing and annoying the teacher because they do not stop talking immediately. Time management can either kill or encourage creativity and as Coleman, Kaufman and Ray write:

> It's a terribly frustrating thing to be stopped when you're in the middle of the process. But we live in such a hurry-up way. So again and again children are stopped in the middle of things they love to do. They are scheduled. There isn't time for children to relax into their own rhythm. (1992: 63)

Resources

This section is dealt with in more detail in Chapter 6. The key point in relation to planning for creative science is to remember that the teacher should not be the 'keeper' of the key to the cupboard. Creativity requires that children are partners in its development and should share some of the responsibility for their own learning. We should therefore develop and expect a level of maturity appropriate to the children that we are working with, which allows them reasonable access to a wide range of resources. In primary education children should develop confidence and skills in using a range of resources and be allowed the freedom to do so. Resources should include books, the Internet, video as well as science equipment including measuring equipment and everyday materials. Developing children's responsibility in relation to equipment and other resources should mean that they do not have to seek for permission or wait for the teacher to organise materials. Where the teacher remains solely in charge, it can result in time wasted for the learner and for the teacher who could be more effectively deployed in the classroom supporting creativity, rather than being the class 'gopher' – going for this and going for that.

Planning for successful interactions

Successful, creative science lessons are those where the children know what they are doing and why, and where the teacher explicitly discusses creativity with children and in his or her interactions praises children in terms of different aspects of their creative thinking and working in science. The teacher should also aim to develop both positive attitudes and motivation towards science and creativity, and help the children to understand how they can improve their own work.

This requires numerous and quality interactions between the pupils and teacher, as well as between pupils themselves. Children should learn that they can also offer praise and encouragement when someone is working well or has an interesting and unusual idea, and participate in commenting as critical friends in a way that encourages learning. Including children in developing quality interactions underlines the holistic nature of creativity and the idea of it being a partnership in which children have a central role.

Planning for high expectations

High expectations are not just about children achieving assessment levels. That is too narrow a framework for creativity to flourish. High expectations are important to creativity. Think of the many scientific discoveries throughout history; they were not based on low expectations from individuals, they were about rising to challenges, solving problems, working co-operatively as well as independently. High expectations that are achievable can be difficult to manage, particularly in a mixed-ability class, unless we separate out the idea of high expectations in terms of content and consider high expectations in terms of learning dispositions in science.

Sometimes children have high expectations of teachers and are disappointed, for example, when teachers do not appear to be listening, or they do not allow children the time to follow through ideas and pieces of work. In terms of expectations, there can be discontinuity between what the teacher expects of a child and what the child thinks he or she is capable of, as the following example suggests.

Teachers are way too overprotective!

Teachers participating in a transition project in Hackney in 2004 carried out a survey of 10–11-year-old pupils who were due to move to secondary school after the summer break. They were asked what they were looking forward to in relation to moving up to the secondary school. One child responded with the following comment: 'More trust from the teachers . . . Year 6 teachers are way too overprotective!'

Developing creativity in science is about having high expectations and making realistic demands on children, but at the same time not underestimating their various social, emotional, academic and creative abilities. Allowing children to take some responsibility and control over their own learning needs to be central to creativity in science. 'A key task for teachers is to help young people to understand these processes and to gain control of them' (NACCCE 1999: 34).

Ofsted (2003: 11) noted that 'Many teachers who stimulate creativity establish a relaxed relationship with their pupils but one in which high demands are placed upon them.'

In some cases, high expectations refers to something quite different, and creative teachers frequently expect their pupils to be creative, 'off the wall' or 'wacky', permitting them to think outside the accepted patterns or 'out of the box', allowing them to take risks. Exemplifying this approach was the primary teacher who told her class: 'The unexpected is expected in my lessons' (Ofsted 2003: 8).

Summary

Creativity in science requires conscious thought on how to present interesting and motivating contexts and how to encourage creativity in the children, working in partnership with the teacher. It may require some schools and teachers to set aside their own concerns about national tests and league tables and be creative in their approach to the science curriculum. This in itself is risky, but belief in the professionalism and ability of staff is important as is the belief that children can and will rise to the challenge presented by creative approaches to teaching and learning in science.

The next chapter considers how resources can support the development of creativity in science and suggests criteria for choosing resources in science.

ACTIVITY SUGGESTION: ICE HANDS

Developing creativity

- To challenge children's perceptions of an everyday material.

- To encourage children to be curious and ask questions.

- To develop children's problem-solving abilities.

Developing science

- To develop children's understanding of changes in state.

- To develop children's understanding of reversible and non-reversible changes.

Resources

ice hands (one between three children)   trays

Language

ice   freeze   reversible   irreversible   change   melt   frozen
water   temperature

Introduction

Take a 'science surprise box' (see Chapter 6) into the classroom and challenge children to ask questions to find out what is inside the box. At the appropriate moment show the children an ice hand. Be prepared for children to be excited; allow them their moment of 'awe and wonder'. Ice hands are made by using rubber gloves, filled with water, sealed with a clip or elastic band and placed in a freezer for at least 36 hours.

Activity

Observing the ice hand

Give each group an ice hand and explain to children that they can handle the ice hand using the paper towels placed on their tables. Explain to the children that their task is to observe the ice hand using their senses and to talk to each other about what they find out about the ice hand. Children who carried out this activity provided many interesting responses, such as:

'It gives me pins and needles because it is so cold.'

'The heat gets between the fingers and melts them first.'

'You can see through some of the ice.'

Asking questions about the ice hands

When children are ready, ask them to clear and clean their table and give them a large sheet of paper. Ask them to draw a large hand in the centre and then write down as many questions as they can think of around the hand. Challenge children to ask questions using different question stems, such as: Which . . .? Could . . .? If . . .? Does . . .?

Children sharing their observations and questions

Allow children to share their observations and questions. Encourage children to reflect on the thinking behind their questions and praise children who ask creative questions and those who use scientific terminology. Here are some examples of questions that children ask:

- What else can we make an ice hand from?

- Why does the little finger drop off first?

- Would the ice hand melt faster if it was chopped in half?

Children answering their questions

Provide children with the opportunity to answer their questions where feasible. The teacher might wish to 'seed' some questions to ensure coverage of the science focus and practical activity. Some questions can be answered as a whole class, for example, children made suggestions about what else they could use to make an ice hand – their responses included jelly, ice cream, squashed bananas, wet leaves, melted chocolate.

Follow-up

Challenge children to think about and suggest ways of finding out:

- What will happen if we leave the ice hand in the classroom for one week?

- Which is the best material to keep the ice hand frozen?

- Which material is the best thermal insulator for a cool bag?

Using resources to develop creative science

 Rainbows are just to look at, not to really understand.

(http://www.juliantrubin.com/kidsquotes.html 12.10.04)

The most precious resource there is in the classroom is the child's mind. To capitalise on the potential of the child's creative mind in science requires the teacher to think creatively in relation to the resources that are used to support teaching and learning. The aim of this chapter is to explore different kinds of resources and how using them can support children thinking and working creatively in science.

The resources that are available and the way that they are used in primary science can either encourage or hinder creative thinking and working in science. Science expenditure in schools is often woefully small and limited to purchasing consumables such as batteries. Schools should audit science resources and use the audit data to create short-term and medium-term purchasing plans. The easy part is purchasing those items such as magnets, bulbs and mirrors, which are the perennial requirements of the science curriculum. More challenging is to be imaginative and be prepared to purchase some expensive items and cheap items from toy shops, not available in catalogues, to support creative science teaching and learning. This chapter offers some guidance on the issues that should be considered when developing resources to support creativity in science.

Choosing resources to support creativity in science

Table 6.1 provides a set of criteria to help science co-ordinators choose resources to support the development of creative teaching and learning in science. One of the greatest difficulties science co-ordinators face is negotiating more funding for science in a financial climate where schools have limited expenditure. It is therefore important to be able to provide the rationale behind various purchases and ensure that, once bought, they are used to the maximum effect.

Once new resources have been purchased, it will be important to remember that, to avoid resources disappearing into the cupboard, a staff inset should be organised to introduce staff to the resources and how they can be used across the primary years in different areas of the science curriculum.

To ensure that resources are used to the maximum to support creativity, the science co-ordinator should consider the following:

- Are staff and children given time to explore resources, get to know them and try them out?
- Have the resources been organised so that children have access to them but understand and work within a system of responsibility – that is, if they take something out then they have to put it away?
- Are children given independence in choosing and using appropriate resources?
- Are teachers and children open to alternative suggestions of how resources can be used?

As adults we will have our own approaches to using resources and therefore have preconceptions on how they can and should be used. Sometimes the teacher will need to put these aside and allow children to be innovative with resources, so it will be important to engage children in talking about resources and encourage them to share their ideas and try things out.

Equally important will be the type of feedback on how resources have been used. The teacher should celebrate creative approaches by asking children to show others how they have used different pieces of equipment and resources. It will therefore be necessary to resist the temptation to say, 'No, that won't work' or 'You cannot use that.' Instead the teacher should be asking:

- How do you think you could use that?
- What do you need it for and how do you think it will help you?
- What other resources could be used instead?

Table 6.1 Criteria for choosing resources to support creativity in science

Criteria for choosing resources to support creativity in science ☺
Will it provide the children with new experiences?
Will it engage and motivate children?
Will the resource interest staff and encourage them to use it in science lessons?
Could it be used to challenge children's ideas in science?
Is it value for money? Is it versatile – can it be used across year groups?
Can it be used to encourage children to use imagination in science?
Does it offer stimulating and interesting experiences?
Does the resource support staff in taking a risk in their teaching?
Will it motivate staff to try different approaches to teaching and learning in science?
Can it be used for different purposes?
Will it provide a 'Wow!' factor in the classroom?

Inviting dialogue about using resources can provide the teacher with access to what the children are thinking. It also allows the children to articulate their ideas and, in doing so, it might lead the children to realise that their idea will not work.

This section illustrates a number of resources that are well known to most teachers, but have been chosen to illustrate their potential in developing creative thinking and working in science.

Body tunic

Often teachers shy away from the expense of purchasing something like the body tunic, but children from early years to later primary are fascinated by it and enjoy using it.

In a nursery classroom, the role play area was a hospital clinic. The children put the tunic on and role played operations, making sure that they put the body parts back in the right place, so that the person wearing it would 'get well'.

Children aged ten used the body tunic to create their own stick-on captions explaining the function of different parts of the body as a revision exercise.

The science Talk Ball

Science revision using this inflatable ball with questions on is a creative and fun way to revise ideas in science. Children throw it around the classroom from one person to another and the person who catches it reads a question out and the class must answer it. There is also a blank Talk Ball so that children can create their own questions, checking the answers and then using the Talk Ball with their friends.

Model skeleton

Some resources are expensive. The skeleton is one that most schools would like to purchase but often do not because of the cost. Card skeletons or a skeleton borrowed from a local secondary school are alternatives. As a resource that has the potential to support creativity in science it can be used:

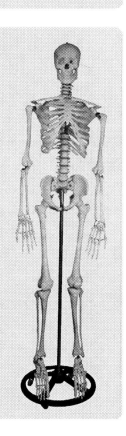

- as an interesting starting point;
- in a hospital role play area;
- to support children creating their own models of the skeleton;
- to support children in writing their own skeleton stories;
- to take digital photographs to label and write captions about body parts;
- for writing songs, poems and rap music about the skeleton;
- as a starting point for surveys on broken bones in children in the school.

Floating magnets

Floating magnets defy expectations. They challenge children's ideas of gravity because the magnets do appear to float in the air. Creativity is about challenging perceptions, challenging children to explain the unexpected. They are a simple, inexpensive but effective resource in getting children to think, offer solutions and suggest how the 'repel' can be used in making their own magnetic games.

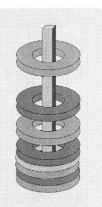

Using children's toys to develop creative thinking and working in science

Developing resources can also be fun and does not have to always depend on expensive purchases. Looking creatively at children's toys can provide some creative starting points for science and resources to support children working and thinking creatively.

Touchable bubbles

As part of a 'six-minute science' session the teacher took into the classroom 'touchable bubbles' which, when blown, can be caught by the children, stacked one on top of the other and stay as bubbles when they land, unlike normal bubbles which burst. The children were excited and quickly managed to catch bubbles, fascinated by their unusual property. The children offered descriptions of what was happening, and their reactions to these strange and exciting bubbles.

When the last bubble had settled, the teacher asked the children what they thought they were made from. Here are some of their ideas.

How did this resource support creativity in science?

Touchable bubbles can be purchased from toy stores. They are cheap and an excellent resource for 'six-minute science' sessions or as a starting point for topics on bubbles or solids, liquids and gases. In terms of creativity this resource:

- offers an experience that is unexpected;

- provides what children would consider an 'awesome' (amazing) experience;

- challenges children's ideas about the behaviour of an everyday material (bubbles);

- is interesting and exciting and therefore motivating;

- encourages children to wonder and ask questions about why the bubbles do not burst;

- can be used to suggest a problem, such as 'could we make touchable bubbles?'

Splob

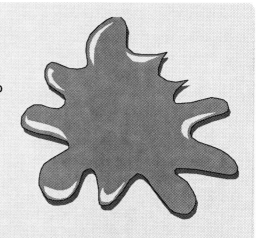

Splob is a playdough-type material which can be moulded and when thrown at a surface will stick to it. The teacher decided to use the Splob as a creative starting point for work on friction. She took some Splob and stood in front of the class moulding it in her hands. The children sat and watched, intrigued, and then the teacher asked them what they would like to try with the material. The answers were various, and all were accepted regardless of content:

'Put it on someone's head.'

'Put it in water.'

'Make a bubble with it, see if it will float or sink.'

Finally someone suggested, 'Throw it!'

Much to the amazement and shock of the children that is exactly what she did. She threw it at the ceiling, where it stuck. Once the hilarity had subsided, the teacher then asked the children, 'What would you like to know about Splob? What really interesting creative questions can you ask?' The children did not disappoint. Here are some of their questions.

How did this resource support creativity in science?

It is amazing how a cheap resource from a toy shop can provide a really stimulating starting point for science. In this vignette the teacher felt that she had a challenging group of children who required a great deal of structure and instruction to ensure that appropriate behaviour in the classroom was maintained.

The teacher thought that her science lessons were 'okay' but fairly pedestrian because of her concerns over classroom management. On reflection she wondered if her approach compounded matters. Pedestrian, highly structured lessons with little input from the children might just be making things worse. So taking Splob into the classroom was a risk. The teacher did not know how the children would react but intuitively she felt that they would be excited and fascinated. Their reaction was a revelation; they were completely intrigued by the substance she was handling and shocked when she threw it. Their concentration and contributions were, by her own admission, fabulous. Why?

- The activity was purposeful.
- The resource and activity were original.
- The starting point for the lesson was unexpected.
- It was within the experience of the children.
- The teacher invited their ideas and questions.
- Children were highly motivated and engaged.
- Both teacher and children recognised what the teacher did was 'risky'.

The Yapping Dog

Alive and not alive is a difficult concept for children, particularly since they take the ideas related to life processes literally. The teacher introduced to young children the idea of life processes and how we could tell if something was alive.

She used the Yapping Dog toy, which is excellent for teaching about living things because it does so many things that a real dog would do; for example, it moves and makes a sound, but of course it is not alive. As soon as the teacher asked questions such as 'Can it breathe or have puppies?' then the children's ideas about what is alive and not alive were challenged.

Why was this a creative use of a resource?

The teacher recognised that teaching the concepts linked to alive and not alive is difficult and children often find it hard to apply the criteria. For example, one member of the class took the idea that things that are alive move quite literally and was convinced that a car was alive because it so obviously moved. Bringing in the Yapping Dog was a creative solution to the problem of how to support children's learning in science. Creativity is not always about the children being creative, but often about the teacher using his or her creativity to think of alternatives to solve a problem. In using the Yapping Dog, the teacher offered something that was intrinsically interesting and motivating to the children, and helped to challenge and move forward their ideas about alive and not alive.

Freedom to use and explore resources

A point made frequently throughout this book is the need to offer children opportunities to be in charge of their own learning. This is much easier in early years where generally the classroom setting encourages freedom and independence. The lessons learned from the example below should be taken throughout the primary years; all classrooms should allow for the freedom to use and explore resources both during and outside of formal science lessons. The demise of the science table in upper primary classrooms has resulted in limited opportunities for children to be curious and try things out. All classrooms should have the facility for children to 'tinker'; in fact all classrooms should have a 'science tinkering table'.

The rainbow

Lucy was four, brimming with questions and curiosity. The class was outside using sunshine and a hose spraying water to make rainbows. Everyone was engrossed in this activity, except Lucy. She knew about rainbows and had brought a book in from home which showed how to make a rainbow using a container, water and a mirror. Lucy knew that those things were available in the classroom and that she had access to them. So she sat to one side in the outside area, determinedly making her own rainbow and after much problem solving with regard to the right angle, persevered and succeeded, with enormous delight on her part, in making a rainbow. So when the class returned to the classroom she eagerly showed everyone how to make a rainbow.

How did this support creativity in science?

In itself one could say that this was not a creative activity, Lucy was following instructions in a book and did not bring any original ideas to the activity. An activity does not always have to be creative in itself, neither do the resources. This activity was important because it helped to develop dispositions that support the development of creativity in science.

Lucy was allowed to explore her own interest and follow through an idea that she had, and had the freedom to do so in her own time. The teacher encouraged Lucy to be independent and find the resources she required, which were available in the classroom and easily retrieved by the four-year-old child. In attempting to make the rainbow Lucy encountered some problems, solved them through persevering and enjoyed her success, giving her the confidence to try something else another time. Lucy also spent time reflecting on her own learning and was happy to explain to others what she had found out and how pleased she was to make it work. As she said, 'It was hard to do, but I did it! Look!'

The science surprise box

The teacher kept in his classroom a science surprise box which was brought out on a regular basis as part of both science lessons and other science sessions. The class knew what the science surprise box meant: they had to ask questions to find out its contents. Used to this game, the children immediately began to fire a range of questions, continually refining them to try to be the first to work out the contents of the box.

In the box the teacher had placed a hard-boiled egg that had been left for several days in white vinegar. The eggshell was soft and squidgy to touch, and the children were both amazed and repulsed by its texture.

How did the surprise box support creativity?

In a classroom where thinking and working creatively is promoted then the children will expect the unexpected from the teacher on a regular basis and look forward to those exciting moments with anticipation. The surprise box was part of children's science; it was a box filled with awesome things, puzzling objects, breathtakingly beautiful things as well as revolting and gruesome objects. The egg in vinegar:

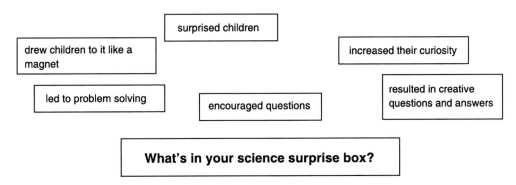

Figure 6.1   The surprise box

Summary

We must remember that sometimes scientific phenomena are intrinsically interesting. As the child quoted at the beginning of the chapter said, 'Rainbows are just to look at, not to really understand.' The teacher needs to provide a range of resources to be used in formal science sessions but also informally by children. We should allow children those moments of curiosity and delight, of awe and wonder.

In Chapter 7 the focus is on how the teacher can support the development of creativity when children are engaged in exploring and investigating in science, building on many of the ideas discussed so far, including the use of different resources to engage children in exploration and fair test-type investigations.

ACTIVITY SUGGESTION: FORENSIC SCIENCE USING EVERYDAY RESOURCES, THE COMPUTER MICROSCOPE AND DIGITAL CAMERA

Developing creativity

- To develop problem-solving abilities.

- To engage children in a creative context.

- To encourage children to be curious and ask questions.

Developing science

- To give children experience of how forensic scientists work.

- To develop children's ability to use evidence to substantiate conclusions.

Resources

computer microscope   forensic items, e.g. hair, fingerprints, soils

Language

forensic   evidence   match   observations   conclusions   pattern   similarities
differences   detective   crime scene   samples   fracture matches   record

Introduction

Children will need to know something about the work of forensic scientists. Ideally a visit from someone either teaching forensic science at a local college or university or working in the field would provide children with the opportunity to find out about this area of science. There are a range of useful websites for lay people which explain issues and practices in forensic science.

Forensic science is wide ranging and entails searching a crime scene, collecting evidence, tagging and bagging evidence, and then analysing evidence in the lab. The forensic scientist deals with a wide range of evidence including fingerprints, DNA samples and even uses dental records to find information. Forensic scientists ask questions, particularly the 'What if . . .?' type. Their work means that they have to pay attention to detail, for example, the soles of shoes tell a lot. They are different, the person wearing them often walks in a particular way which leads to wear on particular parts of the sole. Sometimes they have to look for 'fracture matches' where an item has been torn. Since no two tears are the same, they use a microscope to find out if one material matches the other torn half. Soil can be used to associate a particular scene with a particular individual. Soil can also be used as evidence, for example, soil might be deposited from somewhere else in the crime scene and forensic scientists can match the type of soil and where it comes from. Forensic scientists need to collect evidence, so photographs are an important way of recording aspects of a crime scene as well as taking notes including descriptions, measurements etc.

Activity

Create a crime scene for the children, for example, something has been stolen from the classroom and the thief has left evidence, such as:

hair   torn paper   a paper tissue   shoe tread in soil

Explain to the children that there are a number of suspects and samples of hair, paper, tissue and prints of their shoes have been taken. The children have to consider all of the evidence and using a computer microscope compare the evidence, looking for similarities and creating photographic records to help them build up a case which will prove that one of the suspects was the thief. When they have made their decision, they will have to communicate their conclusion to the rest of the class and use their evidence to convince others they are right.

Follow-up

Children enjoy working as forensic scientists and, once they have worked through their first forensic case, enjoy creating crime scenes with evidence for other children to use.

Thinking and working creatively in science explorations and investigations

 If you are creative you are doing what you think is best. You can make up your own science experiments or something.

(Emily, age 8)

In this chapter the focus is on developing creativity in science explorations and investigations, which is a huge area for consideration. There are many issues and dimensions, too many for one chapter, so this section will focus on the more important areas.

Before we consider creativity in this area, it is important to distinguish between exploration and investigation. Although exploration and investigation may contain similar characteristics, there is a distinction between the two. For the sake of this chapter, exploration is defined as an activity where children are exploring their world through an approach that is 'try it and see'. Familiar contexts for this are the water tray or exploring magnets to see what they can do. For the purpose of this chapter, the type of investigations focused on will be fair test investigations where children are engaged in a more formal framework of fair testing to find an answer to a question or a problem.

The essence of creativity in both exploration and investigation is found in the quotation at the beginning of this chapter. Implicit in the statement by the child is the idea that children should have some degree of independence and responsibility for their actions, and those are based on what the child thinks is best, not the teacher. Ofsted (2003: 11) reports that: 'Many investigations have become highly structured and give insufficient freedom for pupils to contribute their own ideas or reflect on outcomes.'

Both exploration and investigation require opportunities for children to explore their own ideas and seek their own solutions which may require problem-solving approaches. This is at the heart of thinking and working creatively. The teacher needs to provide opportunities for children to engage in exploration and investigation, and those opportunities will have some structure and rationale. However, as De Boo reminds us:

> Young children learn in a more eclectic, holistic way. They do not distinguish between 'work' and 'play', between language development and scientific exploration. Their cognitive learning is bound up with their emotional learning (Beetlestone 1998). Their learning does not occur in a structured linear way. We can stimulate and guide children's learning, but in the event they will focus on what is important, interesting or significant to them at the time. (2004: 10)

The teacher often treads a fine line between providing opportunities for exploration and investigation that provide enough structure for the activity to be appropriate to the topic and the child, yet has enough flexibility to engage and challenge children's personal creativity. The teacher will also need to consider how he or she can engage children in contexts that are creative and, as De Boo (2004: 10) writes, are 'important, interesting or significant to them at the time'.

Starting points for exploration and investigation

This section considers the idea of teachers providing creative starting points for exploration and investigation. Harlen raises the issues of the 'context of activities' and asks:

> Should the science be studied in the context of real life events, which provide interest and stimulate curiosity, but are complex and present ideas often intertwined together, or indeed 'tidied up' activities which demonstrate scientific relationships and concepts in a more direct form but which then have to be related to real situations? (2000: 64)

This chapter advocates the use of interesting and stimulating starting points for science, especially when engaging children in exploration and fair test-type investigations. Not all starting points will be as creative as others in attempting to arouse children's curiosity. When choosing our starting points we should bear in mind the following questions, as offered by Harlen (2000: 67). Does the activity:

- allow children to apply and develop scientific concepts?
- enable them to engage in using and developing scientific skills and processes?
- encourage scientific attitudes?
- engage the children's interest and relate to real life experience?
- ensure inclusivity?
- encourage children to work co-operatively?

Imaginative starting points are important for encouraging children to think and work creatively in science investigations and explorations. There are many options to choose from, some of which are included in Table 7.1 and will be familiar to those engaged in teaching in primary contexts.

Table 7.1 Imaginative starting points for science

Artifacts	Pictures	Videos
Events	Concept cartoons/maps	Internet
Stories	Computer microscopes	CD-ROMs
Poems	Computer programs	Observations
Jokes	Music	Displays
Visits/visitors	Photographs	Collections
Biographies of scientists		

Creative starting points should:

- introduce the ideas;
- be interesting, challenging or unusual;
- invite children to share what they already know;
- draw upon existing scientific knowledge and everyday experiences;
- stimulate discussion so that children share ideas;
- surprise children;
- enable key vocabulary to be identified and used;
- challenge their ideas and assumptions;
- sometimes show something gross (unpleasant) like a mouldy sandwich;
- make them want more;
- be fun.

There is a danger that lip service is paid to using creative starting points, particularly when the follow-up is offered in a rigid, intransigent way that denies children the opportunity to take some responsibility and ownership of their learning. Bruner and Haste (1993), cited in De Boo (2004), remind us that:

> We know from substantial research that children are much more involved in the task, and more competent in devising and using stategies, when they work on problems that they themselves have set. Young children can be very ingenious and inventive in defining a variety of tasks, in directing their own activities with a high degree of motivation and in correcting their errors. (p. 13)

The following is an example of a creative starting point used in an early years classroom. It was developed to offer children a context that provided both structure and freedom for children to follow their own ideas and be creative.

The spider

In the nursery, children had been looking at spiders. They had learned the nursery rhyme 'Incy Wincy Spider' and a display in the setting was imaginative, with large spiders painted by the children, fabric with spiders on and spiders' webs hung around the room.

The teacher decided to develop this interest using the water tray. A range of guttering, drain pipes, drain pipe ends, a watering can and, of course, a plastic Incy Wincy Spider were placed into the water tray.

Brydon, age four, spent his time fascinated by Incy and making the spider move down the guttering and pipes. He repeatedly washed Incy down the guttering which he had positioned so that it went from one end of the water tray to the other. He then placed the spider inside a short piece of drainpipe and placed the pipe in the guttering. Having set this up, he then had 'transport' for Incy sitting inside the pipe. Brydon then washed the pipe down the gutter until the pipe and Incy reached the other side of the water tray, then he repeated the whole process again. (For further ideas related to Incy Wincy Spider, see De Boo 2004: 20.)

Why was this a creative episode?

Firstly the nursery teacher and team reflected on the experiences of children when engaged in water play and decided that a more creative approach was required. They decided that the children needed and deserved more interesting and challenging experiences than were currently being provided. The context of Incy Wincy Spider was motivating, the resources different. They challenged children to explore what they could do with the materials. Children were imaginative in what they did, creating their own mini schema and stories.

This context allowed Brydon and the other children to explore and use their imaginations. They also problem solved, particularly when they were faced with pieces of piping that initially appeared too large for the water tray. In addition, they had to work together and solve difficulties such as fixing different pieces of piping together as well as rescuing Incy when the spider got stuck.

This demonstrates evidence of creative planning from the perspective of the child. Why? Because the child had to constantly make his own decisions about what to do next. Sometimes his actions were instinctive, at other points it becomes obvious to the observer that he was using his personal experience of the pieces of equipment to make something different happen. This is early thinking and working scientifically, where children learn about forces, materials, cause and effect, and being creative in response to the opportunities the context provided.

Indoor and outdoor play and creativity

We should not underestimate the power of offering children a range of opportunities to explore their environment, whether indoors with the water tray or outdoors. Where early years settings have reduced the boundaries between indoor and outdoor activity and a range of multi-sensory experiences are provided, then the opportunities for creative ways of thinking and working are multiplied, but only if the children are encouraged to take the lead.

For many children, school might be the only place where they can 'play' in a safe outdoor setting, where they can explore, climb, dig and take risks. In such an environment children are able to be creative with different materials, space, enjoy different weather, including being out in the rain and snow. Schools should provide appropriate clothing and footwear so that all children can engage in outdoor activity. At home and indeed in some schools many children are called inside when there is light rain or snowfall. In our modern world many children's experience of the outdoor environment is limited in even the most fundamental ways and, as a result, so is their creativity.

Starting points for science investigations

At all ages, most learners enjoy different and unusual contexts for learning. Children in particular enjoy the more 'gross' starting points, where something unpleasant is used to stimulate ideas and imagination. Science should be fun. It should engage all of the senses and at times we should 'assault' the senses, offering experiences that challenge the norm and what we are expecting. Children remember those lessons where the teacher provided or did something unusual. The following is an example of risk taking in teaching, since the teacher does not know what the children's reactions will be and what issues and questions might arise.

The gross lunchbox

The teacher had deliberately left a lunchbox with half-eaten food in it so that the contents would go mouldy. When it was suitably gross, she took it to school to use as an opener for a science lesson on micro-organisms. She did not let the children know what it looked like inside, but asked children what they had for lunch, why they kept their food in lunchboxes and what happened at the end of each day when they took their lunchbox home.

She then told the class that her son had left his lunchbox at school for a week and asked them what they thought it looked like inside. The teacher then opened the lunchbox to show the class the true horror that lurked inside. The children were suitably disgusted and groans of 'gross', 'disgusting' and 'yuk' echoed around the classroom. The class were able to offer suitably disgusting descriptions of what they could see and this led to a discussion on the problems of bringing lunchboxes into school where there are no refrigerated cabinets to keep them cool. The teacher asked the children how they would investigate which was the best place in school to keep lunchboxes and logged their suggestions. Where possible, she allowed them to carry out their ideas.

See *Be Safe!* (ASE 2001) for information relating to moulds in the classroom.

Why was this a creative starting point?

The teacher understood children and their fascination with things that are gross. The contents of the lunchbox were disgusting and children were very motivated and eager to comment and draw on their own experience and scientific knowledge. It led the children into considering issues in their own school related to leaving lunchboxes for several hours in conditions where certain foods, for example, meat and yoghurts, might deteriorate. The children investigated which was the best place for lunchboxes and what kinds of foods would be best in a lunchbox. Above all it was also great fun to have something so disgusting in the classroom!

Lessons where the teacher is prepared to follow the children's lead are often the most creative, where the children are at their most energetic in terms of creativity. The risk is being prepared to move away from preconceived ideas about what questions will be asked and how children might choose to investigate an idea. Many teachers believe this is a risk that they cannot take. However, the risk is actually minimal because the context is set and the resources available usually help to structure what children suggest.

An example is the 'ice hand' (Chapter 5) activity where the teacher asked the children to suggest how they could keep the ice hand frozen. The teacher had expected someone to suggest 'Wrap the hands in something and hopefully place them in a glove.' As adults we know that materials can be used and that some materials are good insulators. Here are some of the ideas that children offered – no one suggested what the teacher had wanted them to!

What does the teacher do? Go with the children's own ideas? Introduce another approach to keeping the ice hands cold? Whatever idea the teacher chooses, he or she must be open to the alternatives and at least engage children in discussing the different ideas, their feasibility and which idea they might be able to try out.

Grossology and creativity

The example of the lunchbox illustrates that the things that amuse children and capture their attention are probably things that are truly gross and we would prefer not to talk about. However, these are often the things that can provide the most fertile ground for engaging children and developing creativity in primary science. The following statements are taken from the London Science Museum website and offer some intriguing starting points for science.

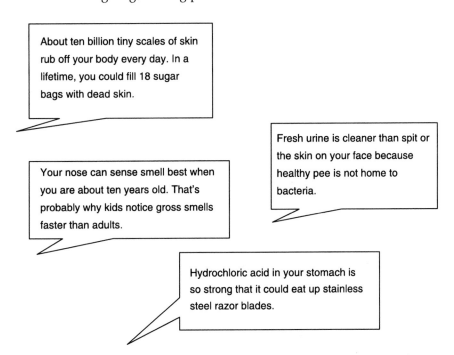

http://www.sciencemuseum.org.uk/exhibitions/grossology/exhibition.asp (17.10.04)

At least two of the statements can be used as a creative starting point for fair test-type investigations. The others could be used to stimulate discussion and research using the web. In both cases an important element is the development and use of personal scientific skills, knowledge and understanding to support creative endeavour. NACCCE (1999: 42) reminds us: 'Freedom to experiment is essential to creativity. But so too are skills, knowledge and understanding . . . But sustained creative achievement involves knowledge of the field in question.'

Stomach acid

Children could investigate household acids such as vinegar and their effects on different materials from coins to egg shell. Investigations could be carried out to find out how different strengths of acid in water affect materials. This could be supported by web quests on acids and the stomach.

Smelly nose

If scientists suggest that children at the age of ten have the best sense of smell, what kind of fair test could children carry out to find out if this is correct? Will they have to test the sense of smell of people of different age groups? Children support their investigation with research on the olfactory system.

Occasionally working with children's interest in the bizarre and gross and taking a risk in engaging with these ideas can be rewarding both for the children and the teacher. As teachers we have to suspend our own concerns and trust in the children. As one teacher suggests:

> Teachers need to lose their own fears and not allow these to hinder the scientific development of the pupils' skills. Don't keep thinking 'What if . . .?', or 'I don't think . . .' or 'These children are not ready . . . or don't have the skills. . . .' Take a leap of faith with your pupils and really learn science together. Let them show you the wonder of science through their eyes and with their enthusiasm, so that one can learn to begin to experience and love science investigations with the same shared sense of joy. (Bukky Yusuf, Teacher and science consultant)

Creative planning frameworks for investigations

Creativity should permeate all aspects of thinking and working scientifically. There are two elements to creative planning:

1 Encouraging children to think creatively when they plan to solve a problem or answer a question.

2 Offering creative planning frameworks to support fair test-type investigations.

Encouraging the children to think creatively when they plan a fair test investigation requires the teacher to:

- Offer problems that are set in realistic, interesting contexts.
- Develop a flexible framework to support children's planning.
- Challenge and support the children to be the decision makers.
- Encourage children to discuss their plans and make changes where appropriate.

For this to be successful and engage children in creative approaches, the teacher needs to:

- Give children 'thinking time'.
- Tell the children that they are expected to be creative and think differently.
- Be prepared to set aside their own ideas of what should happen in favour of the children's.
- Allow children to try out their own ideas – even if it might lead to failure.

The final point in this list is important since in primary science we are in danger of sanitising science and taking out opportunities for children to take risks, problem solve, fail and have to think about and try alternatives. Risk taking is seen as one of the key features of a creative person and therefore children must have opportunities to take risks within, of course, a supportive environment.

Creative planning frameworks

Creative planning frameworks are intended to support children in planning fair test investigations by using a visual framework for children to work with when they plan a fair test investigation. The idea of this type of framework was originally developed by Phipps, Feasey, Gott and Stringer (1996) and is quoted by Feasey in Skamp (1998: 46). The planning frameworks were designed to support children across the primary years, when planning fair test investigations. An example of a planning framework is the planning flower below.

Flower planning framework

Inside the petals of the planning flower are key questions to support children's decision making when planning a fair test investigation. The picture cues the children into the idea that they are planning an investigation about plants and the questions offer prompts for the things that children need to think about.

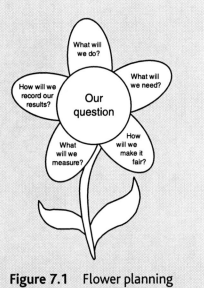

Figure 7.1   Flower planning framework

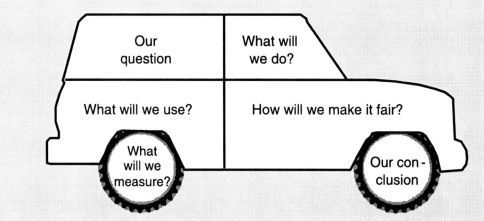

Figure 7.2 Which car goes the furthest?

Figure 7.3 Which sugar dissolves the fastest?

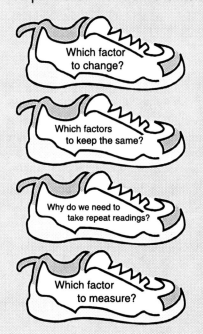

Figure 7.4 Which is the best way to stop the snowman from the melting?

Figure 7.5 Which is the best material for a parachute?

Figure 7.6 Which shoe has the most friction?

Why are planning frameworks creative?

The planning frameworks are a different approach taken by the teacher to cue children into planning a fair test investigation. It is an approach that is:

- different;
- colourful;
- relevant to the context;
- often amusing;
- imaginative;
- risky (where responsibility is given to the children).

The planning frameworks can help to cue children into the context and provide a more interesting way of working than writing into a box-type framework, so often used for planning scientific investigations. More importantly the aim is to focus on the questions in the framework. The pictorial framework may change but the questions remain constant for a period. It is important that the questions relate to the needs and ability of the children. For example, a cars planning framework used in early years to find out 'Which car travels the furthest?' would focus on basic questions about what the children would do, what they would use, how they would make it fair and what they would measure. However, for older children, the shoes planning framework would need to include questions about accuracy of measurement and reliability of results and the demand that children take repeat readings.

Children communicating their science

This aspect is dealt with in more detail in Chapters 8 and 9. The aim of this brief section is to consider that sometimes the teacher will need to think creatively in order to support children in areas in which they are encountering difficulty. Two examples are given: the predicting pegs and text message conclusions. Each one focuses on different elements of thinking scientifically which children find difficult.

Predicting pegs

Very young children, who were exploring plants growing, were asked to think about what a plant needed to grow. The illustration shows how a student teacher offered children the options regarding different ideas they might have in relation to their predictions about what would help their seeds grow.

The student teacher used wooden pegs, each one with the name of a child on it. The children then placed their personal peg on the prediction sheet that showed their idea about growing seeds.

This provided children with the opportunity to communicate what they thought.

It also allowed children to change their ideas as children learned more about growing plants.

Why was this approach creative?

Teachers working with very young children with limited written skills are faced with the perennial problem of how to encourage children to communicate and record their ideas. This approach was a novel and creative response to the need to develop children's ability to predict. It encouraged the children to record their ideas as well as encouraging them to reflect on their own learning (metacognition) and change their ideas as they evolved.

Text messaging science conclusions

Children were having difficulty writing concise conclusions at the end of their science fair test investigation. Two teachers working in parallel classes with eight to nine-year-olds came up with a creative approach to challenging children to think carefully about what a conclusion is and how to construct one sentence about their conclusion.

The teachers gave children an A4 sheet of paper bearing an outline of a mobile phone, which had an enlarged but blank text window. The children were told that they had to:

- Think about their conclusion.
- Discuss it with their talk partner.
- Create a sentence that was short, clear and concise.
- Draft their conclusion on their individual 'whiteboard'.
- Show it to the teacher.
- Rewrite it as a text message on their paper 'mobile phone'.

The class then decided which conclusion they should send and sent one conclusion as a text message using the teacher's mobile phone to the class next door, who were also engaged in exactly the same activity and were busy preparing to send their text.

Why was this approach creative?

The children were highly motivated and worked hard to get their message just right. Why? Both teachers were creative in their approach. How?

- They were not afraid to take a risk.
- They had a specific learning outcome.
- They offered an imaginative alternative for recording results.
- They understood the culture of the children and used it.

Summary

This chapter has attempted to suggest ways in which teachers and children can be creative when engaged in explorations and investigations. At the heart of thinking and working creatively is the need to ensure that the teacher provides a framework in which the children can work, not a straitjacket:

> As teachers we need to provide activities which do not dictate every minute of every lesson about the work pupils do in science. We need to provide opportunities for pupils to express themselves freely about ideas they have. It is only through their ideas being respected that pupils will feel that they have something to contribute to lessons; this in itself will begin to start building independence when managed effectively by us. (Sadyia Kasmi, Teacher and science consultant)

The next chapter considers the role of language in developing creative science and children communicating in this area of the curriculum, and continues the theme of encouraging children to contribute their ideas in different ways.

ACTIVITY SUGGESTION – THE ARCTIC EXPLORER

Developing creativity

- To use and develop children's imagination, giving children problems relating to an alternative environment.

- To encourage children to take risks in their thinking and activity.

- To offer children an opportunity to develop their own investigations and make their own decisions.

Developing science

- To use their understanding of material and environments to problem solve.

- To develop their understanding of how scientists work under extreme environmental conditions.

Resources

websites   outdoor clothing

Language

Antarctic   expedition   explorers   environment   extreme

Introduction

Read the children an extract from the diary of a scientist currently working in the Antarctic or from Scott's diary. Discuss with children what they know about the Antarctic. Create a concept map or log their statements. Suggest to the children that the class are going to prepare for an Antarctic expedition and ask them what they think they will need to know about, for example:

information about the Antarctic   nutritional requirements
types of clothing   keeping fit   moving across ice and snow

Activity

Create different working groups in the class relating to different aspects of life in the Antarctic and explain that each group is in charge of their area. Develop different problems for the groups to explore and find answers, for example:

- Which is the best material for certain items of clothing?

- Which type of clothing will keep the explorers warmest, e.g. gloves, socks, hats?

- What do people in the Antarctic need to eat? Is it the same/different to our own needs? Why?

- Which materials move across an icy surface more easily? How can friction be reduced?

- Which would make a better shelter: an ice house or a tent?

- What do explorers have to think about before going out of their living accommodation?

There are many Internet sites which offer children access to diaries, past and present, of people who have been involved in Antarctic expeditions, and they provide children with excellent information about the living conditions and the daily life of those working in the Antarctic.

www.secretsoftheice.org/expedition

www.bio.research.ucsc.edu/people/williams/Antarctic

www.dailypast.com

www.theice.org/journal

Follow-up

When children have planned their expedition, allow them to take that imaginary journey and dress up, keep video diaries, create their own website.

Language, communication and creativity in science

 I am creative because I always come up with weird names and phrases.

(Alfie, age 8)

The importance of language and creativity in science

Science has its own language: one of molecules and atoms, nanotechnology and anatomy, forces and life processes. Some words trip off the tongue easily; others are technical, long and complex; some, confusingly, also have everyday meanings such as force. Scientific language, depending on your perspective, can be difficult and tedious, dull and incomprehensible, or it can be exciting and puzzling, challenging, beautiful and even fun. Our task as teachers is to help children to develop a love of language, so that they learn to appreciate the beauty and power of words to explore creatively language in science. Wellington and Osborne (2001: 2) suggest that:

1 Learning the language of science is a major part (if not *the* major part) of science education. Every science lesson is a language lesson.

2 Language is a major barrier (if not *the* major barrier) to most pupils' learning in science.

3 There are many practical strategies which can help to overcome these barriers.

Let us examine each of Wellington and Osborne's points in turn. Firstly, learning scientific vocabulary is central to science education. How can children explore and share their ideas and ways of working if they are not able to talk or write about their science? It is therefore crucial that the teacher identifies the scientific (and mathematical) language that children need to use and develop in each topic and lesson and teach the children about the language.

The second point is more controversial and is a matter of perspective. We can either view language as a barrier, and therefore a problem, and assume children will have difficulty, or we can consider scientific language as an exciting challenge for the children and encourage them to learn to enjoy learning new words and their meanings.

Thirdly, Wellington is right to suggest that there are many practical strategies for learning scientific language, the majority of which can be transferred from English and literacy lessons. The important issue here is that the teacher selects the development of language in science as a priority. By building in time during lessons, the children's range of language in science can be extended. Useful approaches that can be used in the classroom include:

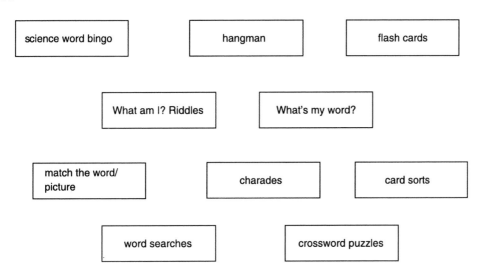

science word bingo

hangman

flash cards

What am I? Riddles

What's my word?

match the word/ picture

charades

card sorts

word searches

crossword puzzles

Learning the language of science should be fun. Creative approaches should be explored and used by the teacher to engage and motivate children. The following is an example of a creative approach to encourage children to learn the meaning and spelling of scientific vocabulary.

Science word shirts

One of the issues in this school was that children were not confident in spelling scientific vocabulary and sometimes unsure of the meaning of some words. The teacher took in her own 'science word shirt' and showed the children how she wrote the word on the shirt, and then drew a picture to show she understood the word. Over several science lessons the teacher added new words to her science shirt that the children had learned as part of their science topic.

She had decided to model how a science shirt was created before she gave the children their own shirt, which they could use for their science vocabulary. The class of seven and eight-year-olds were each given a science word shirt, which were old white shirts donated to the class by parents. The children were told that they could add a science word and picture if they could spell the word and give an explanation of its meaning. The children were keen to learn to spell words and explain the word to their teacher, who then gave them time to decorate their science word shirt.

Why was this approach creative?

Developing children's ability to communicate their science requires children to be able to spell and have an understanding of the technical vocabulary they need to use. As a teaching approach this was creative because it:

- was different;
- offered a personal approach to learning;
- allowed children to design illustrations to accompany words;
- challenged children to learn spellings and construct meaning;
- engaged children's interest.

Descriptive language in science

While it is important for children to be confident in their spelling and use of scientific language, we should remember that science is also amazing, beautiful and awesome and we need to support children in developing the language to describe those qualities. For this reason we need to consider developing children's knowledge and ability to use descriptive words in science and focus on a range of adjectives and adverbs that can support children in describing their experiences in science, and in particular awe and wonder in science.

The use of descriptive language in science is important but not always taught. The tendency is to teach only words such as 'smooth' or 'rough', and not, as children develop their language ability, to increase their vocabulary and offer alternatives. This is not difficult to do; for example, in Table 8.1 below are lists of alternative descriptive words that have been taken from the computer thesaurus. They are all words that can be introduced to children. Their importance is in developing a richness in the language children can use to describe their experiences and emotions in science.

Table 8.1 Alternative descriptive words

Descriptive word	Alternate descriptive words
Smooth	silky, velvety, downy, shiny, glossy
Rough	jagged, irregular, bumpy, coarse, uneven
Awesome	breathtaking, remarkable, awe-inspiring, astounding, humbling
Beautiful	striking, lovely, colourful, magnificent
Gooey	sticky, viscous, thick, glutinous, mushy, runny, gluey
Disgusting	revolting, repulsive, nauseating, repellent, sickening, ghastly

Without a descriptive language base, children will be less effective in communicating their science to an audience. This should be developed alongside children's ability to use scientific terms accurately. However, the ability to use powerful adjectives and adverbs in science is crucial, particularly if children are to develop their ability to communicate creatively in science. For this to happen, the teacher needs to provide children with a range of stimuli involving all the senses and challenge children to describe what they see, hear, taste, feel and smell, using scientific vocabulary as well as a wide range of descriptive words.

To facilitate this, children need to be exposed to effective questioning that encourages them to draw upon different kinds of language. Children should also be exposed to a range of alternative words and their meanings and be encouraged to use them where appropriate. The following is an example of how this can be done.

Spiral, slithering, slimy snail

The teacher wanted to develop the children's ability to use both scientific and descriptive language when communicating their observations. The children were learning about invertebrates and had observed them and found out information about their habitats, feeding, movement etc. The children were given a range of alternative words to use and encouraged to add their own words.

The children were asked the following questions:

What colours can you see on the snail?

Grey, brown, tan, coffee, russet, yellow, gold, green, emerald, olive, bottle green.

What patterns can you see on the snail?

Spiral, speckles, spots, bands, coiled, corkscrew, curved.

How does the snail move?

Slithers, slides, glides, creeps, slinks.

What kind of trail does it leave behind it?

Slime, gunk, substance, goo.

What kind of habitat does a snail live in?

Shady, sheltered, dappled, cool, damp, moist, soggy.

As their vocabulary increased the teacher challenged the children to produce creative alliterations such as sneaky, spiral, slithering, slimy snail.

Why was this approach creative?

This activity was a creative approach to teaching and an opportunity to allow the children to be creative. The children were engaged in an activity that aimed to broaden their descriptive language. Some of the words are fun and trip off the tongue, others are words that children do not usually expect to be allowed to use like 'goo' and 'gunk'. By developing alliteration children are being encouraged to 'explore and play' with language and introduced to the power of descriptive words in science. It is important to break down barriers between curriculum areas, particularly science and literacy. Such barriers are artificial and not useful in developing creativity. Making these cross-curricular links is crucial if standards in science are to be increased. Effective communication in science is essential to scientific literacy. We must therefore consider and use different ways for children to think in science and to communicate their ideas and experiences, focusing on the use of language in science, as well as extending children's experience in language by using approaches such as relevant poetry, plays and stories which are important to science and to tapping into children's creative potential.

As Professor Helen Storey in NACCCE (1999: 85) suggests: 'There are different routes of entry into each child's mind. It is amazing how much can be taught when subject boundaries are taken away.'

Sometimes it is the teacher who needs to find a creative way to encourage children to communicate all or part of their science in a concise and effective way. It might be that children find it difficult to communicate their planning (see Chapter 7), or the teacher wants to understand what they already know and engages children in discussing a concept cartoon (Keogh and Naylor 1997). The teacher may want to focus on an aspect of science such as drawing conclusions in an interactive and interesting way that focuses children's thinking. (An example of this is shown in Chapter 7.)

Communicating effectively and creatively in science

Being literate in science means that children have an understanding of science ideas and ways of working and can communicate these to a range of audiences. Feasey and Siraj-Blatchford state:

> Effective communication demands that individuals are able to communicate to a range of audiences and to act as critical audiences and the development of these skills begins at an early stage. (1998: 1)

A scientifically literate child is confident and articulate but he or she should also be able to tell other people besides the teacher about their science. This will require an understanding that there are many different ways that we can communicate science, for example:

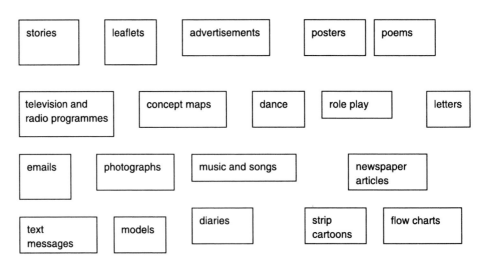

Creative communication in science does not always require the use of the written word. It might be through role play, or use of video or digital photographs. Central to successful communication is an understanding of the needs of the audience which will require children to think about some or all of the following:

- What do they need to know?
- What do I want to tell them?
- How can I make it interesting?
- Which are the most important things?
- What can I leave out?
- What will I use, e.g. pictures, flow charts or a poem?

(Feasey and Siraj-Blatchford 1998: 8)

The audience is an important factor in deciding how to communicate science and children should be offered a wide variety of audiences over their primary career. Children soon get used to the teacher being the audience for their science and soon learn to 'write for the teacher'. Giving children an alternative audience means that the children will have to think carefully about the requirements of that audience and communicate accordingly. They could be offered:

- their peers;
- younger children;
- parents;
- industrial partners;
- partners from the local community;
- governors;
- imaginary characters.

Seed dispersal

Children were engaged in an activity on seed dispersal from Ginn New Star Science Year 5 book, *Life Cycles*. The activity challenged children to research the life cycle of different plants, in particular to find out about seed dispersal. When they had completed their research they had to communicate their science in an interesting way to someone else. Below are extracts from their work.

Beeeeeezzzzzz!

A bee's a flower feeding insect with body hairs,
All the little children and adults it scares,
Bees are dependent on pollen off a flower,
They can collect about 15g an hour.

(Jordan, age 10)

Seeds

I fly through the air,
I'm light as a feather,
I have a tiny parachute,
In the springtime weather.

I have a shiny, juicy covering,
Birds find me very tasty
I come out of the other end,
That way they don't waste me.

I catch a ride on anything passing,
I get carried far away,
I have little hoods that hold on,
On fur I will hopefully stay.

I live in a pod with my siblings,
Some are big and some small,
When it's time to get out,
We all twist then we fall.

(Jessica, age 10)

THE DAILY COUNTRYSIDE 32P

Airman Lands in Country

Two days ago, near the village of Cassop, a family were enjoying a walk when in flew Daniel Dandelion, the famous parachutist, on a mission to disperse his seeds.

He landed in a farmer's field and his seed settled on grass where he is hoping that his seeds will grow soon and it looks like they will, due to sun shining and rain on the way.

by

Countryside reporter

(Chloe, age 10)

Blackberry

I have a juicy covering that helps me as I grow,
The birds, well they eat it, they can't say no.
You know, I can travel miles this way,
I am the blackberry, it only takes a day.

Dandelion

I'm as light as a feather so when the wind can blow,
I use my parachute and away I go.
This helps me to keep in the air,
I am the dandelion yellow and fair.

Sycamore

I've got a wing attached to me,
It helps me spin down from a tree.
The helicopter is my name,
When the wind catches me I'll go spinning again.

(Hiroshi, age 10)

How did this approach support creativity in science?

Children were given the opportunity to find their own creative approaches to communicating their knowledge in science. The examples of children's work indicate that children made creative use of both scientific vocabulary and a range of descriptive language. Importantly the children communicated their scientific knowledge successfully to an audience, and they did so in a creative way.

The language of persuasive argument in science

As children move through their primary education, they will be expected in science to develop the language of persuasive argument. In their investigations, children will need to collect and analyse data, draw conclusions and communicate their findings to others. The challenge for children will be to convince others that the way they worked enabled them to collect valid and reliable data, and that their conclusions are based on their evidence. Children will also need to develop persuasive argument for debate so that they are able to put a point of view across. A number of publications offer approaches to developing persuasive argument, such as Feasey (1998b) and Wellington and Osborne (2001). The following example shows how a teacher challenged children to use their abilities in relation to persuasive argument to develop and assess their ideas of the concept that air is all around us.

Persuading Paul

A class of ten-year-old children were revising the idea that air is all around them. The teacher challenged the children to prove this through writing a letter to an imaginary person called Paul who needed convincing that this idea was true. The children were told that they would have to put together a persuasive argument and use examples to prove that air was around everywhere. Here is an example of one piece of work from a boy in the class.

Dear Paul,

I can prove that there is air everywhere, just in this piece of writing. I wouldn't be writing this letter to you if there wasn't air everywhere. There is even air in a sponge. I have evidence that there is, try it for yourself: get a sponge and put it in a bucket of water, if you squeeze it bubbles come out so there is air in the sponge. Secondly, how do you blow a balloon up if there is no air? Thirdly, take a fish – how do you know that there is air? Well, because of the bubbles that come from a fish. It's not very often that you see a fish with a snorkel!

Can you swim Paul? Because if you can't you use arm bands and if there was no air in the arm bands you would be in a bit of bother. Have you ever seen magicians when they put paper in a cup then dip it in water and it comes out dry? Now that is because of air.

I could go on giving examples for years but I think I have proved that air is real.

Why is this approach creative?

Encouraging the children to write a letter to someone to prove that air exists is in itself a creative approach. It challenges children to think differently about their science and allows them to be creative in their own writing. This child was indeed creative in the examples he chose, the way he 'talked' to Paul in the letter and his use of humour to persuade Paul that air existed everywhere. A key element of the child's response was his use of personal subject knowledge about air and how he used everyday examples to persuade Paul. Creativity is about making creative use of subject knowledge, which the teacher did in relation to science pedagogy and the child did in relation to his own knowledge of air.

In the next example, the teacher challenged children to use a rap song to communicate their personal knowledge about food chains in order to provide two different viewpoints – one from a fox, the other from a tree.

Fox and the tree

A Year 6 class had been learning about food chains, food webs, and predator and prey relationships. The children understood the idea that animals have to find their food while plants make their own food. The teacher suggested to the class that they might communicate this idea through using music, in this case a rap song. He knew that children of this age were interested in music and had some ideas about how rap songs sounded and were put together. The following is an example of one of the songs from a boy in the class.

If only they could talk . . .

Fox: It's all right for you tree. You just stand still. I have to chase my food.
Tree: So, fox, you think I've got it easy, do you? Well, think again . . .
Fox: Yo tree, you're so lazy. I'm much more energetic than you, you see.
Tree: You, dude, you're so darn rude. I'm not lazy – I make my own food.
Fox: Oh, shut your trunk, you're messing with the funk! I run for my scan, get it man?
Tree: By the way, my name's Phil. I use chlorophyll. I still move around. I don't stay still.
Fox: Man, you think you're a chef, but you're really grotesque. You make food, oh yuk!
Tree: I eat healthy food like the way you should. No, I don't eat meat, uh huh!

Why was this approach creative?

The teacher worked with the culture of the children and used a type of music that the children were familiar with and that the boys in particular enjoyed and were motivated to use in their science. It was an unusual approach for the children, which made it even more interesting, and the children were soon engaged in trying to use their scientific knowledge in their rap song. The children were able to use their imagination and step outside the normal parameters set when writing in science.

Summary

The creative teacher will appreciate that children need exposure to a breadth of language as well as different ways of recording and communicating in science. Creative teaching is about ensuring that curriculum links are made seamlessly so that children are not constrained by the boxes that many school systems place subjects into. By allowing children free flow across curriculum areas, in this case science and language, children can develop and use their own skills, knowledge and interest in creative ways in science. A result of creative teaching is creative outcomes from the children who have been encouraged to explore scientific and descriptive language and challenged to use both in imaginative and interesting ways within science.

The following chapter explores the links between science and information communication technology (ICT) in developing creativity, and continues the theme of a seamless approach to the curriculum.

ACTIVITY SUGGESTION: SCIENTIFIC WORD POEMS

Developing creativity

● To develop children's ability to communicate their science in different ways.

● To develop children's use of descriptive and scientific vocabulary.

Developing science

● To develop their ability to use science knowledge and understanding in a different context.

● To revise children's knowledge and understanding of an area of science.

Resources

science word bank for topic

Language

battery   circuit   bulb   wire   switch

Introduction

This activity provides an opportunity for children to revise their subject knowledge in different areas of science through the production of a poem. Discuss with children the idea that they are going to create a poem which takes scientific vocabulary and links it to adjectives.

Activity

Modelling the poem

This example is set in the context of electricity and therefore the children need a set of words related to circuits. These are placed on the whiteboard and the children are asked to reorder them into a logical sequence. Once the sequence has been completed, the teacher asks the children to think of a word or phrase that describes what each of the words does, for example, battery – powers. The teacher then elicits ideas from children for the rest of the words, for example:

Battery	powers
Wires	connect
Crocodile clips	nip

Bulb	glows
Switch	controls
Circuit	works

This provides the basis of the poem, then the children think about a phrase that can be used at the beginning and the end, for example, the phrase, 'In a complete circuit . . .' The teacher then shows the children how it can be used and the poem then is complete.

> In a complete circuit . . .
>
> Battery powers
>
> Wires connect
>
> Crocodile clips nip
>
> Bulb glows
>
> Switch controls
>
> Circuit works
>
> In a complete circuit.

Follow-up

The children could use the same scientific vocabulary but different words. When they have completed their poem, they could produce an illustration to accompany it, for example, a circuit picture or circuit diagram. Other scientific words can be used in a similar way for different topics, such as:

Light – wave – transparent – translucent – opaque – reflect – refract – sun – moon

Plant – stamen – pistil – flower – leaves – stem – roots – ovary – style – anther – filament

CHAPTER 9

The role of ICT in developing creativity in primary science

 Today has been weird – we have done no work at all and it has been really good!

(Jaishree, age 9)

Today's children are the products of a technological age where their world is dominated by technology. Feasey and Gallear suggested that:

> Children at the beginning of the twenty-first century live in a world where they have access to the Internet, digital clocks, digital bathroom scales, video machines and computers which allow children to scan, take and store photographs and desktop publish. Today's children expect to have a mobile phone, to communicate with family and friends, their watches light up and make strange noises and their leisure time is often spent playing complex computer games. Children's lives are surrounded by the products of the information and communication age: children not only live in a technological age, they *are* the technological age. (2001: 5)

ICT is a tool, which can be used creatively in two ways:

1 The teacher using ICT creatively in his or her teaching.

2 Children using ICT creatively in their science activities.

ICT cannot be ignored. Not only have some children begun to develop their technological literacy when they enter school but the whole school curriculum demands that children develop their literacy in the use of ICT. In terms of life skills, ICT is increasingly used in the world of work, home, leisure, government. Competency in ICT is therefore crucial – it will enhance children's own esteem in science and provide them with ways of retrieving, saving, and communicating information and ideas.

The most important aspect about ICT is that it becomes a tool for the children to use. Therefore they need to be trained in its use and have experience of using it and then they should be allowed to decide when, where and how it is used. During their primary education, children should be offered opportunities to use the following in science lessons:

- CD-ROMs
- DVDs
- Internet
- computer sensors

- computer microscopes
- digital cameras
- video cameras
- interactive whiteboard
- television
- tape recorders

The use of ICT in primary science varies. Some schools have a wide range of ICT hardware, while others have a more limited range. In some schools ICT is used as an integral part of science and the children are trained and expected to make decisions about when, where and how it can be used in their science.

ICT and creativity in primary science

The use of ICT in science is not in itself creative. The creative use of ICT in science relies on the interaction between the teacher and the technology or the children and how they use the technology. Interaction is crucial; for example, the interactive whiteboard is only interactive in terms of teachers and children pressing buttons and moving things about. Responses to activities involving an interactive whiteboard can be limiting and children can parrot answers and switch off as easily as they did using an ordinary whiteboard or chalkboard.

However, when used appropriately and creatively by the teacher and the children, there are distinct advantages to using ICT in science. Table 9.1 illustrates the range of uses of ICT in science and their advantages.

Creative and challenging use of ICT can:

- challenge children to use higher-level thinking skills;
- develop a high-level motivation;
- engage children in decision making;
- engage children in problem solving;
- offer creative contexts.

The following section provides some suggestions as to the importance of the different kinds of ICT used in science and some creative applications.

Creativity and the interactive whiteboard

The interactive whiteboard, when used carefully, has many advantages in primary science. For example, it can:

- allow the whole class to see the same material;
- offer large visual stimuli such as photographs, cartoons, video, interactive activities;
- provide opportunities for whole-class discussion;
- encourage discourse, often from quieter members of the class;

Table 9.1 ICT in primary science

Engage and motivate pupils.	Allow children to be in charge of their own learning, e.g. using a digital camera or video, creating a web page or PowerPoint presentation.
Enables access to material that would not otherwise be possible.	Video clips of someone bungee jumping off a bridge as a starting point for discussion on forces or materials and stretching.
Provide quicker and more accurate data collection, saving time and offering ease of access to measure and collect data over periods of time, e.g. temperature, sound and light.	Use of sound, light, temperature, pulse and movement sensors to gather information, e.g. to find out the changes overnight in temperature, light and sound in the school building.
Reduce mechanical aspects of practical work.	Allow children to take computer sensor readings or to create a table and graph using a computer package.
Support concept development.	Children could watch time lapse photography of plant growth to help develop their concepts of life cycles.
Take and store photographs and video clips.	Children could collect digital photographs or video clips of aspects of their environment to study for similarities and differences with other environments or changes over time, e.g. days, seasons.
Enable the classification of information.	Children could use computer data bases that allow children to input data and then sort it according to a range of criteria.
Review and modify their work.	Children's work such as leaflets, posters, letters, reports, newspaper articles can be produced, reviewed and modified more easily than using pencil and paper.
Communicate more effectively.	ICT allows children to communicate in a variety of ways, from emails and faxes to producing PowerPoint presentations or short video programmes.
Enable patterns and relationships in data to be more easily recognised.	Large amounts of data can be collected and stored, e.g. using Excel spreadsheets. The data can then be converted into graphs so that patterns and relationships in the data can be recognised.
Model ideas and simulate situations and phenomena.	Children should have access to a range of programmes that simulate situations, e.g. food chains, day and night, gravity.
Manipulate variables and data.	Computer sensors allow children to manipulate variables, e.g. change light intensity, while computer simulations can allow children to change variables such as gravity so that children can see the effects of the change.

- allow children to make suggestions which can be carried out and then receive instant feedback, e.g. graphs, branching data bases, data loggers;
- encourage children to share ideas, e.g. speech bubbles, written text and concept cartoons.*

(*Concept Cartoon in Science Education CD by Keogh and Naylor)

CD-ROMs and the Internet

There are many CD-ROMs available for children to use. Some offer pictures, video clips, games or activities. The teacher should always question the quality of these resources for the ways they engage the children. The Internet is good in parts. The good educational parts for children are usually national sites created by museums and science centres, television companies and large educational organisations. The more difficult aspects of the Internet are those sites that provide pages of information, activities that are 'recipe-style' and, of course, the fact that children can 'get lost' in the search. For this reason, the teacher should consider developing 'web quests' that inform children where the teacher has located appropriate sites for use.

Graphs, tables and spreadsheets

ICT programmes that create graphs, tables and spreadsheets can be used creatively in primary science. They can be used to help children develop the skills of producing tables and graphs and for handling large amounts of data. It can also be used by children to support them working creatively in science.

The role of ICT in this area is important for the following reasons:

- Computer-generated tables, graphs and spreadsheets help to bypass the difficulty of constructing them by hand.
- Using the computer means that children can move on to data handling much more quickly.
- Children can input 'alternative' data to see what happens.
- Children can see data clearly, ask questions and manipulate data according to their ideas.
- Computer-generated tables, graphs and spreadsheets are so much easier to create and they look better than those drawn by hand.

In using computer-generated tables, spreadsheets and graphs, the tedium of collecting and representing data is taken out of the process and children can have more immediate access to the data in a form in which patterns, trends and anomalies can easily be seen. This in itself is not creative. However, the time that would have been used to draw them can then be put to more creative use in considering the different questions that could be asked of the data.

Computer data loggers

Computer data loggers are an excellent addition to the menu of ICT application available to primary schools. Data loggers should be introduced to children as young as six years old and then used in contexts that become increasingly more complex as children move through the primary years. Like all ICT applications, data loggers require skills in how to use them. They are not, in themselves, creative but the way in which they are used can be. They have much to offer primary science teaching and learning. For example, data loggers can:

- be fun to use – motivation is high when children use them;
- allow children to explore their ideas, manipulate variables (factors) and make links between cause and effect;
- provide instant readings of temperature, light and sound, and movement;
- be important for developing concepts of hot and cold, loud and quiet, light and dark, as well as understanding data;
- convert data into a graph which provides quick and easy access to data handling;
- provide real time data.

Heartfelt moments – monitoring pulse rates

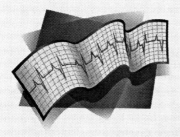

Children aged ten had experienced exploring the computer sensor that monitors and records pulse rate. They knew how to set up the sensor to monitor pulse rate and how to read the data on the graph and tell the story of what was happening to the pulse rate. Children tried various exercises to find out the effect they had on the pulse rate and understood why, after exercising, the pulse rate did not return immediately to its original reading. Their familiarity with the sensor allowed them to be more imaginative with their ideas and questions; for example, they wanted to investigate questions such as:

Why was this approach creative?

The approach taken by the teacher was creative in allowing the children to develop their own questions. The children responded in a creative way, since they:

- asked imaginative questions;
- used their knowledge of the heart;
- asked questions which were based on some unexplored ideas;
- took risks in asking questions that were different.

Modelling and simulation programmes

These programmes offer opportunities for teachers to develop children's understanding of a scientific concept by:

- showing children how something works, e.g. the heart, manufacturing plastic objects;
- modelling/simulating everyday events, e.g. apparent movement of the sun;
- allowing children to offer ideas and manipulate variables and events, e.g. changing the parameter for bungee jumping.

Many modelling and simulation programmes are in themselves very creative. They can be the stimulus for creative thinking about different situations and sometimes be the starting point for children planning and carrying out fair test investigations. An example is where children have watched a simulation of a bungee jumper and are asked to change the variables such as type of rope, weight of person. Then they go on to model this in an investigation.

It is often the questions that these programmes raise that are creative and also where children are encouraged to think about creating their own models.

Digital video camera

There are digital video cameras that are inexpensive and designed for children to use, and these should be available for children to use in science. In schools where the policy is to 'empower' children in relation to ICT, very young children are given opportunities to learn how to use the digital video camera. For example, in some early years settings, four and five-year-old children are given a video camera to film their friends exploring in the sand or water tray. They are then given time to show their film to other people, both adults and children in the early years setting, and are encouraged to talk about what is shown on the film.

Digital video camera

A class of eight-year-old children, familiar with using the digital video camera, used it to video a fair test investigation that they were carrying out and provided a commentary on:

- what they were doing;
- how they were keeping their test fair;
- what happened;
- their conclusion.

Why was this approach creative?

In this school, this teaching approach by the teacher is creative. Why? Because it is different; the teacher is taking a risk allowing the children to work independently and engaging them in a different way of communicating their science. However, in a school where children are already confident and independent users of ICT across the curriculum and where they are expected to make decisions about when to use ICT, this approach would not be different or a risk for the children and therefore not a creative teaching approach. However, the outcome might be very creative, because the way in which the children use it might be very creative in terms of how they decide to use the video camera in science-based activity. In this example, the children were very creative in this lesson; they decided which aspects to focus on, they were creative with the language they used, taking the role similar to television commentators. The children also reflected on their work and critically evaluated their commentary and the quality of the film as they worked.

Children need to be encouraged to communicate their science in ways that are interesting and motivate them to be creative in their approach. Why is this creative? Children can:

- choose their own way of communicating;
- make decisions about what to video;
- explain things in a more interesting way.

We must remember, though, that creativity is relative. Often teachers will change their practice to a more creative way of working in relation to their own approach. Then, in time, the new approach becomes an accepted part of their teaching repertoire.

Computer microscopes

Children can now have access to computer microscopes that are designed specifically for use by children of all ages. Many computer microscopes enable the children to:

- view images through a computer;
- view images on an interactive whiteboard;
- store digital photographs;
- store digital video clips;
- create time lapse photographic sequences;
- print photographs;
- add text;
- use the photograph to create patterns and altered images.

Most computer microscopes designed for use by young children are so easy to use that children quickly become experts and with encouragement from the teacher begin to explore creative uses of these microscopes in science. Where children are given access to a computer microscope to use themselves, research shows (Feasey, Gair and Shaw 2003) that they follow a similar learning path. Children:

- explore their bodies using the computer microscope;
- collect things from around the room and from outside to view under the microscope;
- are eager to share images with other people – peers and adults;
- want to teach others how to use the computer microscope;
- want to return to the microscope throughout the day.

Teachers involved in research for the British Educational Communications and Technology Agency (BECTA) collected comments from children who used the Intel Computer Microscope. Here are some of their comments, all of which are testimony to the interest and motivation the computer microscope generated.

It was fantastic because you could do all sorts of things.

It's ace!

Seeing things more closely was brilliant.

The hardest part was the video but once I knew, it was brilliant and I liked making videos the best.

Today has been weird – we have done no work at all and it has been really good!

Headteacher, I shrunk the class!

A sponge might not be the first thing that you think of as interesting and likely to intrigue children. The teacher, though, used a computer microscope to show children what a sponge looked like and the children were fascinated. Many of the children in the class had English as an additional language and were often reluctant to contribute to discussions. However, the children were animated and offered many comments on their observations. So successful was the observation that the teacher extended the work by asking children to imagine that she had by magic shrunk them to a minute size, so small that they could fit inside the sponge easily. They were then asked to describe being inside the sponge, what it felt like and what happened to them, showing an understanding of the sponge as a material and the forces involved.

Inside a sponge

I was 2cm tall. I was trapped inside a sponge.
Inside it was soft and swiggy.
It was like a bouncy mattress.
It was quite slidey inside as well.
It was like walking on air because when you stood down the air was just shooting up at you. It looked like a soft brain, but brains are hard.
I came over to a big hole, I didn't know how to get over.
I slid down to the bottom of the hole. Then I climbed over some rocky sponge. I found some holes so I can put my feet in and I jumped and bounced along like being on a trampoline.

(Caitlin, age 7)

Why was this approach creative?

The teacher used the computer microscope and the interactive whiteboard to show an everyday object from a very different perspective, which in itself was creative. The teacher wanted to show the children a viewpoint that would challenge the children's ideas of the sponge, which was seen as a boring and uninteresting object. In doing this, the teacher herself was creative in looking for other qualities in everyday objects and changing her teaching approach to use two new pieces of technology simultaneously.

In using this approach, she was prepared to encourage the children to share their ideas and was willing to 'go with the flow', unsure as to where the children might take the learning and her teaching. This in itself is an example of risk taking by the teacher. As the lesson progressed, the teacher recognised the level of interest in the different view of an everyday object and took another risk by changing her plan of the lesson, extending it to include a descriptive literacy element, asking children to imagine they had been shrunk to fit inside the sponge.

Desktop publishing (DTP)

There are many DTP packages that allow children to communicate their science creatively. As children's experience and ability in using ICT develops, they should be encouraged to use ICT to communicate their science creatively. In order to do this successfully, children must be encouraged to:

- use their scientific knowledge;
- research new scientific knowledge;
- use scientific language;
- use interesting language;
- think about their audience;
- be creative in their ideas;
- take risks and try out new ideas;
- explore different kinds of formats and applications.

The following is an example of children using DTP to communicate knowledge and understanding of plants.

Positively passionate about plants

In this activity 10–11-year-old children carried out research on plants using the Internet. The teacher decided that in order to avoid children 'downloading' verbatim information about plants the children should be challenged to create a 'fact file' using their DTP skills. The children were encouraged to think about:

- what the audience needed to know;
- how to make the page interesting;
- being creative in their work.

Ferns

Ferns have thin veins that run through them to feed the plant with water and nutrients.

Ferns are plants that live mostly in damp forests, under trees.

The leafy branch of a fern is called a frond. The small leaflets that make up the frond are called Pinnae.

The Life Cycle of a Fern:

This is what a fern needs to survive:

Moisture in the soil;

Moisture in the air;

Suitable nutrients;

Sufficient light for photosynthesis;

Suitable temperatures;

Protection from wind and protection from too much sunlight.

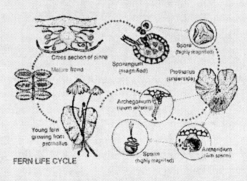

FERN LIFE CYCLE

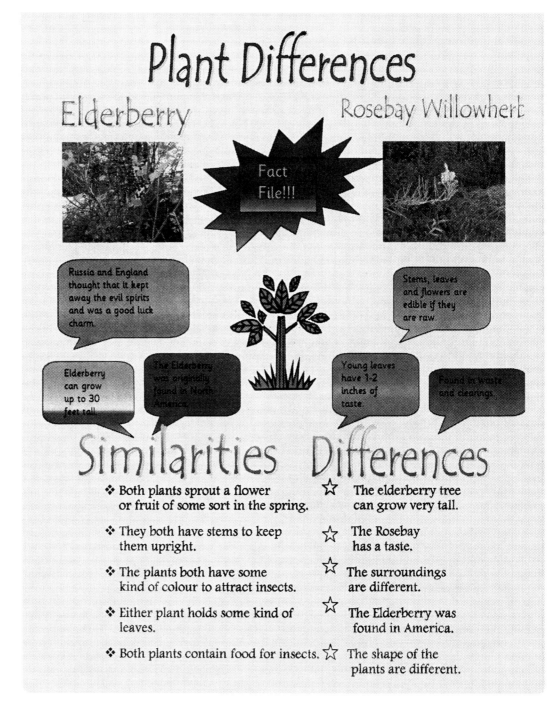

Why was this approach creative?

This approach was creative in two ways. Firstly, the teacher offered children a different way of communicating their science which drew upon a range of abilities across the curriculum, including their science, language and ICT skills. The teacher encouraged the children to be 'creative' in their approach, which gave them a clear message about the quality of the work they were to produce, but it also gave the children 'permission' to try things out.

Secondly, the children were creative in their approach and made good use of their understanding of how to engage an audience in their fact files, by including text, pictures, different headings, and using a range of colours and layout styles. Ultimately children should have been exposed to a range of ICT and its uses across the primary years, so by the end of their primary career children are able to choose which type of ICT would be the most appropriate to use and be able to use it confidently and creatively. In the following example, children were given a problem which they investigated and were asked to communicate their investigation to an audience in a creative, yet appropriate way.

Accidents in the home

The children had been given a letter from the Royal Society for the Prevention of Accidents (ROSPA) with information that the lastest craze for laminate flooring had resulted in more accidents in the home. Some of the accidents were caused by people wearing socks and slipping on the floor; others were due to people not using grips to keep rugs fixed on the laminate. A number of the accidents were caused because people were wearing shoes and slippers where the soles were too smooth and therefore had limited friction. ROSPA was asking for help in investigating this problem.

The class investigated the soles of different shoes to find out which had the most friction and considered which material would be best for slippers. This work was also linked to a design and technology activity in which the children were challenged to design and make a pair of slippers. The children used their findings from their science investigations and subject knowledge to inform the designs of their slippers.

One group of children rose to that challenge using PowerPoint, digital photographs and a computer graphing package. (The still screens from the PowerPoint presentation unfortunately do not do justice to the skill of the children in the creative use of different customised animations to make the presentation more interesting for their audience.)

a

b

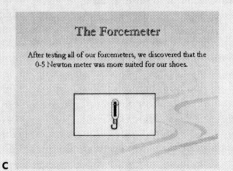

c

d

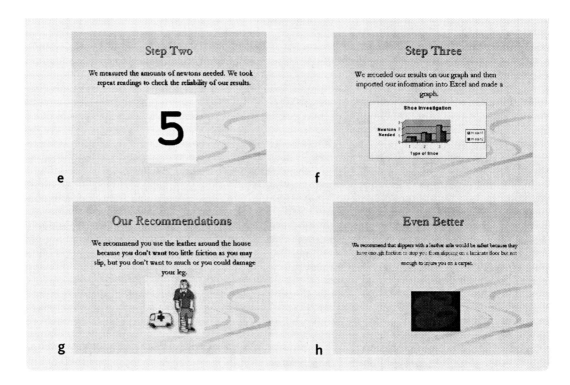

Why was this approach creative?

ICT gives children access to writing about science in interesting ways which, when completed, can, even for young children, look very professional. In this example, the children were able to use their ICT skills to communicate their scientific thinking and ways of working imaginatively. The children made their own decisions, were creative in their approach, had an understanding of the needs of the audience and aimed to keep their audience interested through using animation and humour.

Creativity and international collaboration in science

The advent of the Internet has provided the opportunity for children to experience the world as a global village by allowing them to communicate with children from other countries and cultures. De Boo (1999: 155) comments that: 'the expanding potential for enquiries and communication via the computer opens up the children's world from school to school (electronic mailboxes) and worldwide (the Internet)'.

She goes on to suggest that school linking via the Internet is important to minimise the isolation of some rural schools and to encourage the exchange of information, data and results from investigations in science. This mirrors how scientists work in the modern world where they communicate to share ideas, ways of working and results with colleagues in many different countries. This is the science community at work, and email and the Internet helps to break down international barriers. Scientists can work creatively with someone on the other side of the world on a daily basis and children can also do this in their science.

Why is this a creative approach?

Working collaboratively in science with children from another location via the Internet offers immense possibilities, and schools which work in this way are being creative in their approach by offering children opportunities to develop their creativity. They are also allowing children to experience working in a way that the national and international science community now takes for granted. This approach can help to develop creativity because children:

- may have to take leaps of the imagination to visualise the context children from another country are living and working in;
- have to consider their audience when communicating to someone from another country and culture;
- may be exposed to creative ideas and ways of working used by someone else;
- can pose problems and work together in ways that may demand creative solutions.

Summary

ICT is a powerful tool that opens many doors for children to think and work creatively. For most children, ICT is inherently motivating and once children develop appropriate skills they can explore their creative abilities in many different directions. Sometimes they become so engrossed in using ICT that it does not feel as if they are working – as the child quoted at the beginning of the chapter said.

In the final chapter, the focus is on science fiction, which might be considered as the final frontier of creativity in primary science. It has yet to be explored by many teachers as a route into teaching and learning creatively in science. The contents of Chapter 10 should offer convincing evidence that science fiction is worth exploring by teachers and children together, extending their creativity in ways not usually used in the primary curriculum.

ACTIVITY SUGGESTION: SENSING OUR SCHOOL – A LIFE IN THE DAY OF . . .

Developing creativity

- To encourage children to generate creative questions to answer.

- To challenge children to communicate creatively to an audience.

Developing science

- To develop their ability to use ICT in a science context.

- To be able to collect, analyse data and communicate the story the data tells.

Resources

computer sensors   video camera   digital camera   tape recorder

Language

sensors   data   analyse   evaluate   fields   time periods   frequency   readings

Introduction

Explain to the children that they are going to tell the story of a 'life in the day of' their school through the use of computer sensors. Ask them to think about how data sensors can be used, drawing upon their knowledge of having used them in previous science activities. Then ask the children to consider a typical day at school and what happens. List their ideas. Then ask them to think of interesting questions that they could ask, for example, about sound, movement, light and temperature around the school. Their questions could include:

- Are some classes noisier than others? Why?

- Why do some teachers wear jumpers, cardigans or jackets and others stay in short-sleeved tops?

- Why do some classes keep the lights on all day? Why do some classes keep the blinds closed? What would the classroom be like if the blinds were kept open?

- Which is the noisiest part of the day? Why? Which is the quietest? Why?

Children should also be challenged to think forward to the finished product – a video, PowerPoint, school web page – to ensure that they collect the necessary evidence as they work. The children might be given specific questions to answer, and the whole class might pool their information to create a broader picture of the school day.

Making sense of the data

The children will have to make sense of the data they have collected, for example:

- How valid and reliable is each set of data?

- What relationships might there be between data sets, e.g. data on light and temperature?

- How can they interpret the data in relation to human movement around the school?

- What science knowledge and understanding can we use to make sense of the data, e.g. the apparent movement of the sun and light temperature data?

- What implications does the data have for the school? Do some classrooms need carpet because the movement of people and furniture makes those areas noisy? Are some classrooms too hot? How could the school conserve energy?

Communicating their findings

Issues such as interesting and creative approaches to communicating to an audience should be discussed and children encouraged to 'tell the story' in ways that they personally find interesting and can best use their ICT skills, or indeed extend them.

Follow-up

Children should be given the opportunity to show other people their product. This might be other teachers, children, a teacher from the secondary school or a school governor. Where an audience is offered, the audience should be briefed in its role, which should be to engage with the content of the communication and respond with comments and questions.

The outer limits: creativity and science fiction

I like science fiction because I like science and technical things.

(Jack, age 8)

In this final chapter, the focus is on the use of science fiction in the primary curriculum. Science fiction is a genre of literature less frequently used in schools, perhaps because it is not seen as mainstream reading material. However, science fiction is the epitome of creativity and it belongs to science. It provides examples of creative attributes such as:

- using the imagination;
- taking risks;
- solving problems;
- extending boundaries.

Science fiction is where the writer engages in 'mental play' with scientific ideas and moral issues facing communities, whether they are human or of another world. Science fiction can be fascinating and exciting, frightening and often worrying in its portrayal of future worlds, yet can also be full of humour. In relation to the ideas about creativity offered by the children, science fiction fulfils many of their criteria; for example, it allows children to:

- let loose the imagination;
- be encouraging and joyful;
- let the imagination run wild;
- be creative and daring;
- reach new heights;
- think the unthinkable;
- be mind-boggling.

Science fiction deserves the attention of the primary curriculum, in both science and literacy. This chapter shares the ideas and work of children engaged in activities related to science fiction. Nicholas Fisk, Philip Reeve and other science fiction writers, be afraid! The next generation of creative science fiction writers may be here on these pages.

What is science fiction?

There are many definitions of science fiction. Clute (1995: 6) defines science fiction as 'Any story that argues the case for a changed world that has not yet come into being is an SF story.' It is a genre of fiction where the authors ask 'What if . . .?' and where they use their current knowledge and understanding about science and technology to create a story. Today's science fiction authors have an abundance of science topics to base their writing on, such as space travel, other worlds, time travel, robots, genetic engineering and nanotechnology. Many of these help to pose moral and ethical issues which have yet to be resolved. Science fiction, as opposed to science fantasy, is written to a set of loose criteria, some of which are:

- Science fiction is about 'a world'.
- It argues world changes.
- It is consistent with the language of assumptions and arguments – if A happens then it follows that B can happen.
- It is based on science fact.
- It allows for thought experiments.
- Science fiction extrapolates the future from the present.

Why should science fiction be included in primary science?

Perhaps the best people to answer this question are the children themselves. Here are some responses from a class of 8–11-year-old children as to why they like science fiction.

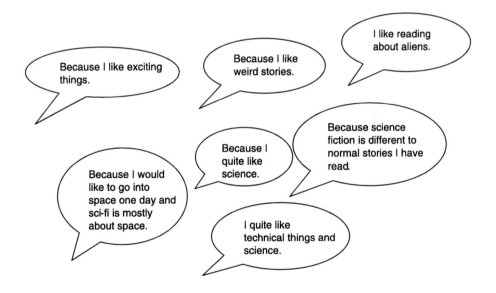

Science fiction should have a special place in primary science. Not only is it creative and engaging for both girls and boys but it allows children to be involved in 'thought experiments' where they can use their science alongside their imagination to truly 'think the unthinkable'. At the same time, it challenges children to:

- consider a world that is different from the one they live in today;

- consider some of the moral and ethical issues facing the human race, e.g. what it would be like if everyone was the same (cloning);

- consider consequences, that is, if they change something then it may cause something else to happen;

- use their personal scientific knowledge and understanding to underpin what they are writing about.

Science fiction and the future: the year 5000

A mixed year group of 8, 9, 10 and 11-year-olds had been looking at science fiction and understood how science fiction stories were constructed, i.e. using scientific knowledge to write fiction. They were asked to think about what life might be like in the year 5000. The children were challenged to consider different aspects of life, from the environment to homes, clothing, school and leisure. The teacher had discussed the idea that if by 5000 there had been a major change in the environment then they should think about how it would affect different aspects of life. Here are some of their ideas.

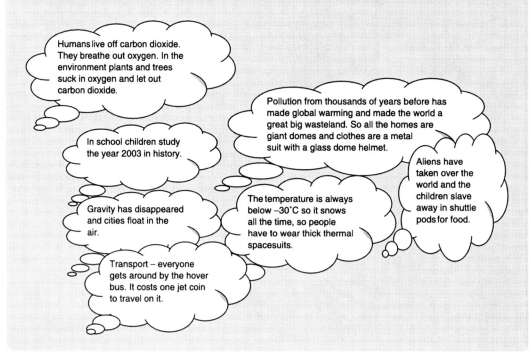

Why was this activity creative?

It allowed the children to use their current knowledge about life on Earth today and extrapolate to a scenario in the future. It demanded that they made links with their personal scientific knowledge, which is one of the criteria for a creative person, then apply it to let their imagination run wild and think the unthinkable. The children were motivated and interested in exploring their own ideas and deliberately worked to be creative.

Science fiction and 'What if . . .?'

The question 'What if . . .?' is an important one in writing science fiction. Many authors pose this question in relation to a whole range of topics, for example:

What if we were able to travel forward in time?

What if we could colonise Mars?

What if aliens landed on Earth?

They then construct their story around the consequences of the actions.

Children were given 'What if . . .?' cards and asked to create a story in response to the question. They were reminded of the important features of a science fiction story:

- It had to be based on science.

- It was a story – fiction.

- It had to be mind-boggling.

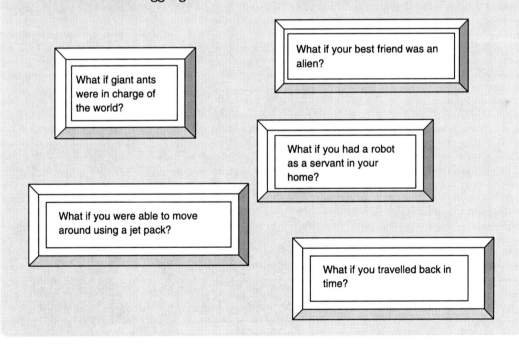

Why was this activity creative?

In the activity, the children had to write a story where:

- it was fiction;

- it was based on scientific knowledge and understanding;

- they were challenged to think through consequences – if that happens, then this might be the result;

- they had to solve a problem;
- they offered novel solutions;
- they were encouraged to reach new heights in their own thinking about their own and other worlds;
- they were allowed to let their minds run free and be daring – think the unthinkable.

The Time Table

'As she tidied her magazine away in the table drawer she noticed three coloured buttons: red, amber, green. Below them were three signs: past, present and future. Thrilled with excitement, she pushed the red button that said, "PAST". There was no going back now. A whirlwind of blues and reds swirled around her head. She had gone back 500 years. She had reached her destination, the high cliffs above the sea. In the distance she could see silhouettes. Not knowing what they were, she ran towards the strange shapes . . . How was she going to get the dodos back to the future?'

(Rachel, age 10)

The story about travelling back in time and finding a dodo was continued and the character in the story took a dodo back to her own time in the hope that she could revive the dodo from extinction. She encountered many problems and finally realised the impossibility of trying to keep a dodo alive in her bedroom (and a secret from her mother), so decided to return the dodo to its own time.

The story below was also about travelling back in time but to a land of the dinosaurs. The child was excited by the idea of being given 'permission' to think the unthinkable, and asked of the teacher, 'Is this really creative?' What do you think?

The Spiral

'I saw a little spiral appear in the middle of the room. At first I thought I was seeing things, so I decided I would just walk through it to prove it was my imagination. I walked cautiously towards the spiral. It stayed where it was. Suddenly I ran nervously towards it and jumped into it. I emerged into a prehistoric jungle or at least something like that. I heard a rustling in the trees. Then a huge bush started moving violently. A very big animal that looked like a hugely enlarged lizard with big, roughly triangular plates on its back appeared out of the bush. You would immediately realise it was a stegosaurus but I didn't know very much about dinosaurs. I thought it wanted to eat me. Stegosaurus (unless you already know that) only eat plants. Anyway it was charging towards me. It must have thought that I was an absolutely delicious great big bush. I looked back, the spiral was still there. I dived through it exactly at the same moment as the stegosaurus hit me.

(Daniel, age 8)

Why was this activity creative?

There are many reasons why this is a creative activity and why the children's responses were creative. Firstly, their work is entertaining, a story well told, with excellent use of descriptive language and a sense of audience. The children followed the basic rules of science fiction writing and successfully used scientific knowledge in their work. They clearly engaged in 'mental play' and enjoyed the freedom of thought, knowing that they were expected to think differently in their writing. The parameters were set by the teacher and the children were given time to think about their story, permitting a gestation period in which ideas were shared, changed and refined. They were encouraged to be creative and discussed what that would mean, in terms of thinking differently, not being afraid of their ideas or of sharing thoughts so that they could listen to themselves.

War of the Worlds

This final example is based on children reading a piece of science fiction as part of an English lesson. One of the most well-known science fiction books was used, *War of the Worlds* by H.G. Wells. The teacher introduced an extract from the text and the children read it, discussed it, considered science fiction as a genre and examined how Wells used language to convey a range of emotions and how he managed to create a picture in the reader's mind of chaos and fear. The children were then asked to write in the style of H.G. Wells and here are two examples of work from ten-year-old children. Like Wells they created descriptions that are powerful, used language in a creative way to convey emotions and draw the reader into a world of unspeakable horrors.

War of the Worlds – the war

'I stood in despair as the tall, brown-skinned alien slithered along the common towards me. My fear increased dramatically, I turned, to see everyone else fleeing to some nearby trees. Everyone, that is, apart from the struggling shopman. Stumblingly, I followed the others, tripping over my own feet as I did so. Blood-curdling screams could be heard from miles around, as the alien moved closer to the trees where people had found refuge. I ran as fast as any man has ever run but the alien was too fast for me, as I felt a slimy gorgon tentacle wrap around my legs. I could feel the creature lifting up my body into the air. He carried me to the crater in which the cylinder had crashed. I was taken inside the ship and was pushed down next to the shopman, who had also been captured.'

(Joshua, age 10)

The Ambush

'I could not avert my face from these things. Loathsome was the word that came to me. The Thing advanced towards me. I turned and ran. But ungovernable tiredness had affected me, and I fell. Home would be my refuge, so I picked myself up and ran on. A dauntingly long shadow appeared behind me as I neared my home. People were running back and forth and tumultuous wails could be heard from all directions.

Injured people were scattered around me and, like arrows, the others darted to safety. I slowly turned. Indescribable terror gripped me. The sound of the raging thing echoed from tree to tree. My flesh crawled.'

(Andris, age 10)

Why was this activity creative?

The teacher introduced the children to a role model for creative writing related to science. Science fiction offers power and drama as a genre of literature, and Wells shows the awesomeness of science and portrays the potential horror of a war of the worlds.

Extracting one of the more powerful parts of the book introduced children to writing science fiction and the teacher challenged them to consider how it was written, using powerful descriptive words and phrases. She encouraged the children to 'get inside' the mind of the writer and then asked them to attempt to convey the awfulness of the scenario.

At all times the teacher held high expectations of the children, and they also worked to their own personal expectations and drafted and redrafted their work, until they were happy that the standard was appropriate for them.

Most importantly the teacher developed an understanding in the children that science and fiction can go together.

Summary

Children have amazing minds. Their creativity knows no bounds if it is allowed to flourish. One of the most important factors in the development of children's creativity is the teacher; most importantly, a teacher who is willing to develop his or her own creative capacity, in order to facilitate children striving to reach their own creative potential. We must therefore ask ourselves what kind of teacher do we want to be? Does the word 'creative' feature in our answer? For the sake of generations of children, it must in order that primary science teaching and learning are scintillating, fun, reach new heights and allow children to think the unthinkable.

ACTIVITY SUGGESTION: ALIEN EGGS

Developing creativity

- To use and develop children's imagination.

- To encourage children to take risks in their thinking.

- To provide children with an opportunity to engage in 'mental play'.

Developing science

- To develop their ability to use science knowledge and understanding in a different context.

- To develop children's ability to engage in persuasive argument.

Resources

computer microscope photograph of, for example, rice crispies

Language

alien   risk   argument   consider   evidence   future   scientists

Introduction

Develop the context where children are in role as leading world scientists who have found 'alien' eggs and have to decide whether or not to allow them to hatch. Explain to the children that they are going to have to consider the arguments for and against hatching the eggs because they will have to take part in a debate on this issue.

Activity

Preparing for the debate

Divide the class into half, one half arguing for allowing the eggs to hatch, the other for not allowing the eggs to hatch. The children have to develop their points for arguing their point persuasively. The teacher might need to provide children with a range of words and phrases which they can use to create their argument for or against. Children could work in small groups and each group would be given two or three minutes to put their case to the rest of the class. Alternatively the class might take part in an open debate where groups can counter the arguments made by others.

The debate

Discuss with children the rules for the debate. Ask children to think about and then share their ideas about how the debate should be conducted. Decide on a set of rules that might be placed on a whiteboard as a reminder of what has been agreed.

Make sure that as children engage in the debate, they remember that they should aim to be quality communicators and a quality audience.

Quality communicators make sure that they:

- use the language of persuasive argument;

- are clear in their presentation;

- address the audience.

A quality audience:

- listens;

- does not interrupt;

- engages mentally with the issues offered by the person speaking;

- thinks about a response.

Follow-up

Follow-up to the debate could be in the form of the children creating a newspaper article which summarises the debate, giving both sides of the argument so that the reader can come to their own decision. The children would have to think about:

style of reporting   attention-catching headline

content of article   photographs

References

Association for Science Education (2001) *Be Safe!* (3rd edn). Hatfield: ASE.

Beetlestone, F. (1998) *Creative Children, Imaginative Teaching.* Buckingham: Open University Press.

Boden, M. (1992) *The Creative Mind.* London: Abacus.

Bruner, J. and Haste, H. (eds) (1993) *Making Sense: The Children's Construction of the World.* London: Methuen.

Carr, M. (2001) *Assessment in Early Childhood Settings – Learning Stories.* London: Paul Chapman.

Chawla, D.R. and Pole, C.J. (1996) *Reshaping Education in the 1990s: Perspectives on Primary Schooling.* London: Falmer Press.

Clute, J. (1995) *Science Fiction – The Illustrated Encyclopedia.* London: Dorling Kindersley.

Coleman, D., Kaufman, P. and Ray, M. (1992) *The Creative Spirit.* New York: Penguin.

Davies, D. and Howe, A. (2003) *Teaching Science and Design and Technology in the Early Years.* London: David Fulton.

De Boo, M. (1999) *Enquiring Children, Challenging Teaching.* Buckingham: Open University Press.

De Boo, M. (ed.) (2004) *The Early Years Handbook – Support for Practitioners in the Foundation Stage.* Sheffield: Geographical Society.

Duffy, B. (1998) *Supporting Creativity and Imagination in the Early Years.* Buckingham: Open University Press.

Feasey, R. (1998a) *Primary Science and Literacy.* Hatfield: ASE.

Feasey, R. (1998b) 'Effective questioning in science', in R. Sherrington, (ed.) *ASE Guide to Primary Science Education.* Hatfield: ASE.

Feasey, R. (2000) *Science Is Like a Tub of Ice Cream – Cool and Fun – A Collection of 100 Poems by Primary and Secondary School Children.* Hatfield: ASE.

Feasey, R. (2004) 'Creative futures'. *Primary Science Review,* **78,** 21–33.

Feasey, R., Gair, J. and Shaw, P. (2003) *Evaluation of the Intel Play QX3 Microscope.* Research Report to BECTA. University of Northumbria.

Feasey, R. and Gallear, B. (2001) *Primary Science and Information & Communication Technology.* Hatfield: ASE.

Feasey, R., Goldsworthy, G., Phipps, R. and Stringer, J. (2003) *New Star Science – Six Minute Science.* Books 3, 4, 5, 6. Oxford: Harcourt Education Ltd.

Feasey, R. and Siraj-Blatchford, J. (1998) *Key Skills: Communication in Science.* Durham: Durham Associates Ltd.

Feldman, D.H. (1999) 'The development of creativity', in J. Sternberg (ed.) *Handbook of Creativity.* Cambridge: Cambridge University Press.

Fisher, R. (1990) *Teaching Children to Think.* London: Blackwell.

Frost, J. (1997) *Exploring Science and Technology: Creativity in Primary Science.* Buckingham: Open University Press.

Gardner, H. (1993) *The Unschooled Mind – How Children Think and How Schools Should Teach.* London: Fontana Press.

Guildford, J.P. (1975) 'Creativity: a quarter of a century of progress', in I.A. Taylor and J.W. Getzels (eds) *Perspectives in Creativity.* Chicago: Aldine, pp. 37–59.

Harlen, W. (2000) *The Teaching of Science in Primary Schools.* London: David Fulton.

HMI (2004) *Ofsted Subject Report – 2002/3 Primary Science.* London: HMI.

Hollins, M. and Whitby, V. (2002) *Progression in Primary Science – A Guide to the Nature and Practice of Science in Key Stages 1 and 2.* London: David Fulton.

Keogh, B. and Naylor, S. (1997) *Starting Points for Science*. Crewe: Mill House Publishers.

McBer, H. (2000) *Research into Teacher Effectiveness. A Model of Teacher Effectiveness*. DfEE Report.

Monk, M. and Osborne, J. (2000) *Good Practice in Science Teaching – What Research Has to Say*. Buckingham: Open University Press.

NACCCE (1999) *All Our Futures: Creativity, Culture and Education*. London: DfES.

Nichol, L. (1998) *On Creativity/David Bohm*. London: Routledge.

Nickerson, R.S. (1999) 'Enhancing creativity', in J. Sternberg (ed.) *Handbook of Creativity*. Cambridge: Cambridge University Press.

Ofsted (2003) *Expecting the Unexpected: Developing Creativity in Primary and Secondary Schools*. HMI, 1612 e-publication.

Phipps, R., Feasey, R., Gott, R. and Stringer, J. (1996) *Star Science Teachers' Resource Book*. Aylesbury: Ginn & Co.

Sherrington, R. (1998) *ASE Guide to Primary Science Education*. Hatfield: Stanley Thornes.

Siraj-Blatchford, J. and MacLeod-Brudenell, I. (1999) *Supporting Science, Design and Technology in the Early Years*. Buckingham: Open University Press.

Siraj-Blatchford, J. and Siraj-Blatchford, I. (1995) *Educating the Whole Child – Cross-curricular Skills, Themes and Dimensions*. Buckingham: Open University Press.

Skamp, K. (ed.) (1998) *Teaching Primary Science Constructively*. Southbank Victoria: Harcourt Brace.

Sternberg, J. (ed.) (1999) *Handbook of Creativity*. Cambridge: Cambridge University Press.

Wallace, J. and Louden, W. (eds) (2002) *Dilemmas of Science Teaching – Perspectives on Problems of Practice*. London: Routledge Falmer.

Wellington, J. and Osborne, J. (2001) *Language and Literacy in Science*. Buckingham: Open University Press.

Websites

http://www.ofsted.gov.uk/publications (accessed 18.7.04)
www.ncaction.org.uk/creativity (accessed 15.06.04)
http://www.nanotec.org.uk/finalReport.htm (accessed 14.08.04)
http://www.sciencemuseum.org.uk/exhibitions/grossology/exhibition.asp (accessed 20.10.04)
http://www.juliantrubin.com/kidsquotes.html (accessed 06.09.04)

Index

Printed in the United Kingdom by
Lightning Source UK Ltd., Milton Keynes
137183UK00007B/27/A